Nature Puzzlers

Nature Puzzlers

Lawrence E. Hillman

1989
TEACHER IDEAS PRESS
A Division of
Libraries Unlimited, Inc.
Englewood, Colorado

TEACHER IDEAS PRESS
A Division of Libraries Unlimited, Inc.
P.O. Box 3988
Englewood, Colorado 80155-3988

Library of Congress Cataloging-in-Publication Data

Hillman, Lawrence E.
    Nature puzzlers / Lawrence E. Hillman.
    xiii, 152 p. 22x28 cm.
    Includes bibliographical references.
    ISBN 0-87287-778-7
    1. Natural history--Study and teaching. 2. Educational games.
3. Puzzles. I. Title.
QH51.H54 1989
508'.0712--dc20   89-27512
                                                  CIP

Contents

NATURE PUZZLERS II
MODERATELY DIFFICULT

NATURE PUZZLERS III
DIFFICULT

Acknowledgments

Although many people have contributed to the final version of *Nature Puzzlers* (including untold numbers of students), I am especially indebted to several people whose encouragement and expertise made this book possible. First, I would like to thank Harmon Alpert, a high school biology teacher in the Mapleton School District of Adams County, Colorado, for his patient classroom testing of the puzzles and his enormously valuable suggestions. Our numerous discussions over a period of several years regarding problem-solving, inquiry, and the art of teaching science became the backbone of this project. Second, I would like to thank Key Levinson, reading teacher at Central High School in Aurora, Colorado, for her criticism and evaluation of the student handouts. Her insights into the reading needs of students, especially those with reading problems, were an invaluable resource in creating the student material.

In addition, I would like to thank the staff at Libraries Unlimited for their help and encouragement. I would like to thank, in particular, David Loertscher for his helpful advice and creative input, especially with regard to information concerning the use of library media centers. Finally, I would like to thank Judy Matthews for her help in obtaining some of the illustrations and Susan Sigman for her patience in answering my many questions.

Introduction

One of the wonderful aspects of using inquiry methods in the classroom is that anyone can do it—yes, anyone! Many people, however, are reluctant to try inquiry as a strategy because of the shroud of mystery that surrounds the process. Many teachers feel that inquiry methods are only for those who can wade through the glut of scientific research with its formidable jargon. This same feeling is similar to that of science students who think that scientific knowledge is the result of some magical process to which only the intellectual genius is privy.

Actually, the only key to doing inquiry is to *do* inquiry—lots of it. Inquiry can be done at any level of sophistication. Some teachers feel most comfortable beginning with simple games and then gradually developing more detailed approaches. Others already are familiar with particular models, such as Suchman's inquiry model or Taba's model of inductive inquiry, and use these as examples for building their own systems of teaching. (For more information on these models refer to *Models of Teaching* by Bruce Joyce and Marsh Weil, New York: Prentice Hall Inc., 1980.) Still others enjoy using highly sophisticated models such as those developed by the Biological Sciences Curriculum Study or the Philosophy for Children program. Some teachers are happy experimenting with loosely structured problem-solving activities in which students discover their own cognitive strategies. All of these systems "work" because inquiry is a natural process that proceeds even if the teacher simply "gets out of the way" and guides the activity only when appropriate.

When presented with a sufficiently interesting problem, students normally begin with a strategy that can be diagrammed as follows:

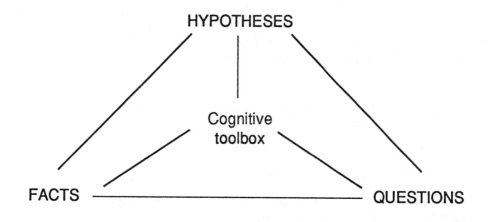

Inquiry may begin on any vertex of this triangle. The student may begin by postulating a series of tentative hypotheses, by collecting relevant facts, or by asking some necessary questions. Any one of

Libraries Unlimited, Inc. • P.O. Box 3988 • Englewood, CO 80155-3988   *Nature Puzzlers* (Lawrence E. Hillman)

these operations naturally leads to the others. For example, if a student begins with collecting facts, some of these facts may lead to questions, which in turn may result in the formulation of some possible hypotheses. These new hypotheses may then result in a search for new facts, which might raise additional questions, and so forth. Mediating this activity is the student's "cognitive toolbox"—the student's existing set of cognitive problem-solving skills. For example, some students possess only rudimentary skills in generalizing or making simple inferences. Other students are more advanced. They are able to use metaphorical thinking or long chains of deductive reasoning to reach conclusions. These "toolbox" skills enable students to refine the processes of questioning, explaining, and fact-finding—thus furthering inquiry. A list of these cognitive skills is discussed later in this Introduction.

What is the teacher's role in this process? Writers on this subject have used words such as "guide," "catalyst," "nurturer," and so forth, to describe this role. One can quickly glean from this vocabulary that the teacher is a facilitator of cognitive growth, not simply a source of information. This role as facilitator does not imply that the teacher should never provide facts or concepts. However, it does mean that the teacher asks questions, provides connections between ideas, assists students in finding information, and identifies correct and incorrect reasoning. The teacher adds to the student's toolbox of cognitive skills by helping each student to identify his or her particular problem-solving strategies and to develop new strategies. Teaching these cognitive skills one at a time often makes the activity strained and seemingly irrelevant to the student. When strategies are identified and modified during the course of solving interesting problems and then reinforced in the course of solving further problems, the skills retain their meaning and relevancy.

Another advantage of identifying skills during a "natural" problem-solving activity is that students learn new strategies from other students. By observing the strategies of fellow classmates at work on a problem, students expand their own set of skills. This expansion of skills is particularly evident when the teacher asks students to identify their own thinking processes out loud as best they can. The teacher can then help students understand the processes through clarification and explanation.

For many teachers, one of the major obstacles to bringing inquiry into the classroom has been finding a significant number of "problematic situations" with which to confront their students. Not every problem situation satisfies the criteria necessary for inquiry. The puzzle or problem requires a specific set of characteristics that foster further cognitive growth. The criteria for each puzzle are as follows:

1. It should be intrinsically interesting or unusual enough to create some cognitive dissonance in the students' minds.

2. It should be presented in an interesting way.

3. It must be challenging enough to promote sustained inquiry.

4. It should be nontechnical enough to draw on a common base of knowledge but detailed enough to foster the discovery of new concepts or facts to expand that knowledge base.

5. It should involve both familiar and unfamiliar cognitive skills.

6. It must be solvable by students of various levels of ability.

7. It should be flexible enough to accommodate various teaching styles.

The development of *Nature Puzzlers* involved a conscientious attempt to satisfy these criteria. First, each puzzle was chosen from the real world of nature. Although some puzzles are written as fiction, the scientific facts contained within each puzzle are true. Second, puzzles were selected to reflect something either unusual in nature or a common natural object or event that could be viewed in an unusual way. Third, each puzzle was designed to be readable and interesting. A reading consultant previewed the puzzles for readability and interest; classroom testing substantiated the belief that the puzzles can be used over a wide range of grade levels and abilities. Since little or no technical science background is needed to solve the puzzles, they may be used for grades seven through twelve. Technical concepts that develop during the course of solving the problem can be adapted to grade level. Thus, criteria 1, 2, 3, 4, and 6 from the above list are satisfied.

Criteria number 5 was satisfied by including puzzles that show a wide range in level of difficulty. Some puzzles, for example, can be solved rather easily by persistence in fact-finding (although some other skills may be cursorily involved). Other puzzles are more difficult and require a number of higher level cognitive skills. Still others are challenging enough that whole teaching units can be developed around them. The puzzles in this text are grouped according to level of difficulty—from simple to more complex.

Criteria number 7 was more difficult to meet. This criteria required the creation of a book that was not a simple-minded set of "recipes." Instead, it required a dedicated effort *not* to think for the teacher. Each puzzle begins with an introduction to the teacher followed by a series of suggested additional activities. The introduction and additional activities are possible avenues for inquiry. An assumption is usually made that the teacher knows more about his or her own students than any other person. The teacher is encouraged to use these suggestions only as a springboard for creativity. Therefore, the introduction or "teacher's key" to each puzzler provides valuable information concerning the puzzle. The key enables the teacher to ascertain quickly what the puzzle is about, which cognitive skills are important in solving the puzzle, which content areas or concepts are related to the puzzle, and the level of difficulty. This key is followed by suggestions for ways to use the puzzle, additional background information, the solution to the puzzle, the experiences of teachers who have tested the puzzles, alternate hypotheses, and suggestions for additional activities.

The suggestions for additional activities take into account various teaching styles, disciplines, and grade levels. These activities are not labeled according to grade level, discipline, and so forth. The teacher can use these activities as appropriate for his or her students. Furthermore, some additional exercises provide a means for the teacher to evaluate his or her students' acquisition of concepts and cognitive skills.

A good general procedure for the teacher to use with *Nature Puzzlers* in the classroom might be as follows. (The teacher may want to refer to the sections on using the library media center and using cognitive skills of this Introduction for help in preliminary planning.)

1. Begin by reviewing the importance of learning inquiry skills. Show their relevancy to everyday affairs. If particular skills are to be emphasized, explain these skills in more detail.

2. Preview the students' knowledge base about the objects of inquiry—such as specific facts about the animals or plants in the puzzle.

3. Have students read the puzzle. Then, ask the class as a whole to complete the Fact-Question-Hypothesis Worksheet (see page 14). Encourage students to list on the worksheet as many facts, questions, and hypotheses as they can from reading the puzzle. Student responses can be acquired through discussion, library research, and brainstorming. The completed worksheet becomes the basis for further inquiry.

4. Evaluate the students' responses and participation. For example, assign a point system for completing the worksheet. Encourage students to write down ideas as they come to them during the lesson, particularly if they did not have an opportunity to present them during

discussion. Use the students' notes for further evaluation. Require students to write down all facts, questions, and hypotheses presented—not just their own.

5. Begin a search for new relevant facts. The search for additional facts is usually suggested by hypotheses and questions that have been listed by the students. Some teachers may want to assume that certain facts are true and proceed as if they were. Others may want the students to research these facts more rigorously.

6. Evaluate several of the suggested hypotheses on the basis of the facts collected. Here students will use inference, deduction, and a number of other higher level cognitive skills to aid in determining the most reasonable hypotheses. This aspect of the inquiry also will generate new questions, searches for new facts, and so forth. During this time, ask many questions, point out new strategies, evaluate students' reasoning, and generally act as mediator to the discussion.

7. The worksheet titled "Hypothesis Worksheet" (see page 15) can be used as an optional student form for comparing hypotheses in detail. The hypotheses may be the student's own or a listing of suggested ones from the class. Guide students through the process of evaluating hypotheses several times before they attempt to do so on their own.

8. When the puzzle has been solved to the satisfaction of both the teacher and students, use the suggested additional activities to reinforce certain skills developed during the course of the inquiry and any concepts or facts that were discovered during the activity.

Remember, this procedure is only a suggestion. It will be modified often as the inquiry progresses. Since inquiry is a self-correcting procedure, it does not lend itself easily to a simple step-by-step approach. Therefore, the teacher must keep in mind that the "Teacher's Key" for each puzzle is an informal summary of possibilities intended to aid the teacher in facilitating students' ongoing strategies. As the teacher uses the puzzles, he or she will develop further questions, add to the number of possible hypotheses, identify new cognitive skills, and evolve new strategies for each puzzle.

Nature Puzzlers offers a great deal to many teachers in the areas of cognitive skill development and the introduction of new concept areas to students. One of the most important things it offers is a fun way to learn! The puzzles are instant discussion starters. Teachers who have tested *Nature Puzzlers* in the classroom report that students enjoy reading the puzzles and enthusiastically bring forth explanations, questions, and facts from their own experiences. The author developed these puzzles in his own science classroom over a period of many years and reports the same enjoyable and educationally rewarding experience.

Libraries Unlimited, Inc. • P.O. Box 3988 • Englewood, CO 80155-3988   *Nature Puzzlers* (Lawrence E. Hillman)

Using the Library Media Center

An extremely valuable aspect of *Nature Puzzlers* is the optional use of the school's library media center (LMC) to develop students' skills in finding, handling, and recording information—skills in which many students are sadly lacking. Each puzzle suggests an information search for relevant facts, theories, and examples. This search provides the teacher with the opportunity to work closely with the LMC to enhance the cognitive skills developed in the classroom.

With some advanced planning with the LMC personnel, the teacher can optimize library use. The following series of questions can be used as a guide for such planning. Of course, not all of these questions are pertinent to every puzzle or activity. Furthermore, some overlap exists between the skills suggested in this section and those in the following section, using cognitive skills. However, if the teacher plans carefully, redundancies can be minimized and the library's resources can be used efficiently.

RESOURCE QUESTIONS

1. What resources are immediately available at the school LMC?

2. Is interlibrary loan available?

3. What possibilities exist for networking or on-line searches?

4. Can local experts be called upon for information?

5. Do local or government agencies provide relevant information?

6. Can the LMC personnel suggest other resources not mentioned above?

SEARCH QUESTIONS

1. How does the information search begin?

2. Do students work individually or in groups?

3. Which resources are used first?

Libraries Unlimited, Inc. • P.O. Box 3988 • Englewood, CO 80155-3988   *Nature Puzzlers* (Lawrence E. Hillman)

4. What sources of frustration might students encounter?

5. Are students familiar with book and periodical indexes, tables of contents, and so forth?

6. Can specific search strategies be recommended to students to aid in the search?

7. To what extent do students develop their own search strategies?

8. Are students able to scan information effectively?

9. Are students asked to find pictorial examples of a concept?

10. At what point is the search for information ended or deemed adequate?

INFORMATION HANDLING QUESTIONS

1. Can students distinguish between primary and secondary sources?

2. How are "authorities" identified?

3. How is the accuracy of information determined? Is the information current?

4. How are conflicting facts, theories, and opinions handled?

5. Can several information sources be combined to provide a single answer?

6. Can students distinguish between factual and narrative sources?

7. How is information classified or categorized?

8. Can students distinguish between fact and opinion, fact and inference, and so forth?

9. How do students distinguish between relevant and irrelevant information?

10. To what extent do students need to recognize unstated assumptions?

RECORDING INFORMATION QUESTIONS

1. How are sources cited?

2. What is the final product of the search—written reports, audiovisual presentations?

3. How is plagiarism handled?

EVALUATION QUESTIONS

1. How do students evaluate themselves? "What facts and/or skills did I learn?" "What do I need to improve?"

2. What types of evaluation does the teacher use?

Using Cognitive Skills

The following is a description of the cognitive skills that may appear during the course of solving *Nature Puzzlers*. Each skill category contains a short explanation of the skill, some eliciting questions that can help the teacher guide students in understanding the skill, and an example. The list is divided into frequently used skills and less frequently used skills. This division is not entirely arbitrary; it reflects the experience of teachers who have used the puzzles in their classrooms. However, "less frequently used" should not in any way be interpreted as "less important."

FREQUENTLY USED SKILLS

Questioning

This skill is extremely important because it usually guides the direction of the inquiry. In addition to asking the "who, what, where, when, why, and how" questions, the teacher should encourage students to recognize the difference between questions that can be answered by facts, questions about the meaning of terms, and rhetorical questions. Students gradually will learn that the type of questions they ask will determine the type of answers they receive.

When a student asks a question, the teacher should ask how the answer to that question may be obtained. Can the answer be found in a book, by experimentation, in a dictionary, by general agreement?

Example:

Student: How does the owl carry the snakes back to the nest? Don't their claws kill the snakes?

Teacher: How can we find out about owl talons?

Defining

Students often have trouble with new vocabulary that arises during an activity. This difficulty is particularly true for words that have both a common and a special scientific usage—terms such as "aggression" and "territory." The teacher should never assume that students agree on the meanings of terms used in the puzzle or in discussion. Discussions about particular definitions can be enlightening to both teacher and students. Students need an opportunity to understand that defining involves more than simply looking up the term in the dictionary. The process of defining a term involves skills such as supplying instances of a concept, visual aids, setting classification boundaries, avoiding circularity, setting criteria, and defining a concept by physical operations such as measuring. Notice that a close relationship exists between defining and concept formation. The resemblance is not accidental.

The teacher can approach the meaning of terms by asking questions similar to the following: "What do you mean by such and such?" "Are you defining a concept or an object?" "What is an example of such and such?" "What is an example of something that is not a such and such?" "Is this such and such like a so and so?" "Can you measure a such and such?" "Can this term have different meanings under different situations?"

EXAMPLE:

Teacher (in dialogue with students):   "What do you think a 'community' is?" "Where does a community of people begin and end?" "Is a city a community?" "Is your neighborhood a community?" "Are all neighborhoods communities?" "Can you have a community without people?"

Hypothesizing

This skill requires that the student form an hypothesis or explanation that is relevant to solving a puzzle. A good hypothesis has several characteristics.

1. It is clearly stated.

2. It is testable either through observation, fact-finding, or experimentation.

3. It is relevant to the demands of the problem situation.

Students quickly learn to distinguish between a useful hypothesis and one that leads to a dead end. An example of a poor hypothesis might be, "The owl carries snakes to its nest because it wants to." This hypothesis is unclear in its terms, nontestable, and probably irrelevant. The teacher should point out to students that some poor hypotheses can be "repaired" by making closer approximations to the above criteria. For example, if the student suggests that "the reason the owl is bringing snakes back to the nest is because the snake is doing something for the owl," then the teacher may respond by asking the student to explain what that "something" might be.

In general, the three best eliciting questions for teachers to use during the process of formulating a hypothesis are as follows: "Can you be more specific about ...?" "How can the hypothesis be tested?" and "How, in detail, does your hypothesis explain the puzzle?"

EXAMPLE:

Student: I think the owl is bringing snakes back to the nest for the babies.

Teacher: OK. That's a good start, but let's see if we can make your hypothesis even better. What would the baby chicks do with snakes?

Student: Eat them.

Teacher: Good. Now restate your hypothesis so that it includes that information.

Student: The owl brings the snakes back to the nest so the babies have something to eat when they hatch.

Teacher: That's very good. Now how can you test this hypothesis? What about the facts given in the puzzle? Is there any fact in the puzzle that is not explained by this hypothesis?

Induction

Induction is the process by which one infers a general rule or principle from a number of specific instances. Consider this example: "Tony dropped three passes in today's football game. He cannot catch anything but a cold!" This example shows that inductive reasoning is always a tentative and risky business. The teacher should remind students constantly that inductive reasoning is to be used carefully and that they should search diligently for counterexamples.

In the classroom, this skill usually emerges in several ways:

1. The teacher asks the students to form a general principle from a set of instances.

2. The teacher asks students to recognize an instance of inductive reasoning used by someone else.

3. The teacher asks students to refute a general principle by providing counterexamples (refuting an overgeneralization).

EXAMPLE:

Student A: Owls eat only snakes.

Student B: No they don't. I saw an owl on television that ate mice.

Teacher: So some owls eat snakes and mice?

Student C: They eat other birds, too.

Teacher: What can you say in general about what owls eat?

Student A: They're meat-eaters.

Teacher: Has anyone ever heard of an owl eating a plant? Can we say that all owls are meat-eaters? How can we find out?

Deduction

Deduction is the process of drawing a conclusion by reasoning. Deduction may involve drawing a conclusion from a single premise or from a series of premises. An example of a conclusion drawn from a single premise is as follows: "All birds have feathers. Therefore, a robin has feathers." An example of a conclusion drawn from a series of premises is as follows: "If an object is more dense than the liquid in which it is placed, the object will sink in the liquid. Therefore, an object more dense than water will sink in water. A piece of granite is more dense than water. Therefore, a piece of granite will sink in a lake."

Libraries Unlimited, Inc. • P.O. Box 3988 • Englewood, CO 80155-3988   *Nature Puzzlers* (Lawrence E. Hillman)

In the classroom, students will normally draw conclusions silently and then present the results of their thinking to the class as a terse statement. The teacher should ask the student to recapitulate the thought processes leading up to the conclusion, then discuss the correctness of the thought process with the student. The teacher may want to write the student's premises and conclusions on the chalkboard so that other students can provide input. For incorrect deductions, provide counterexamples or examples with a similar deductive form that are obviously false. The following are good questions to ask students: "How did you arrive at that conclusion?" "Can anyone see a reason why this conclusion might be false and give some examples?" "Can anyone give some examples of similar types of reasoning using different concepts and facts?"

EXAMPLE:

Student A: If a person has appendicitis, they have pains in the stomach. Right?

Teacher: Yes, ordinarily.

Student A: If John has stomach pains, then he must have appendicitis.

Teacher: Class, does this reasoning seem correct to you?

Student B: You can have stomach pains without having appendicitis. It happens all the time.

Teacher: How about this example? If my car runs out of gas, then my car does not run. I think we agree on that. But what if I turn this sentence around? If my car is not running, then it must be out of gas.

Student C: You can't switch around the two parts.

Teacher: What do you mean?

Student C: You can't turn the sentence around keeping the "if" and the "then" in the same place without making the new sentence false.

Teacher: That seems to be true in this case. Are there times when you can turn it around and still have a true sentence?

Fact-finding

Fact-finding is an absolutely essential skill for survival in the modern world. Observation, library research, and experimentation are the most frequently used methods of finding facts. However, many students are often severely lacking in one or more of these skills.

Questions such as "What do you see?" "What are the main ideas or concepts?" "How can we find the information we need?" "How do you know this fact is important?" "Why is it important to know this fact?" help students make progress toward attaining these skills. The teacher should emphasize that fact-finding is not a random process but rather is guided by the questions and hypotheses developed in solving the puzzle. In this way students begin to see the relationship between these activities. They also begin to understand how one makes distinctions between relevant and irrelevant facts.

EXAMPLE:

Student A: The graph on the puzzle says the death rate from heart attack and pneumonia went up in the years 1890, 1918, 1919, and 1929. So we ought to find out what happened in those years, right?

Student B: Lots of things happened in those years. We can't find out everything that happened.

Teacher: She's right. We're going to have to limit our search somehow.

Student C: Maybe we should learn about heart attacks and pneumonia first.

Teacher: Those are still pretty big topics. Maybe we need to ask some questions that can guide our research. What kinds of questions might help us?

Assuming

All thought involves assumptions. The problem is that most of the time assumptions remain hidden under the guise of "common sense." Unfortunately, false assumptions can highly restrict our abilities to solve many problems. As a result, the teacher must help students identify, justify, and correct assumptions when necessary. A good way to begin an inquiry about assumptions is with an example: "You are assuming such and such. What else are you assuming?" If students are exposed often enough to recognizing their assumptions, analyzing their assumptions becomes a matter of habit. In fact, on occasion, "assumption bashing" has degenerated into a game of one-upmanship in the classroom—exposing each other's unjustified assumptions first and with devastating logic to boot. If such intellectual games are not carried to extremes, they can be beneficial to the student.

EXAMPLE:

Student: We think we've listed all the factors that affect the growth of a plant—light, wind, rain, soil, and other plants.

Teacher: That's a pretty good list. But it's not complete.

Student: We've thought of everything! What else could affect the growth of plants?

Teacher: Aren't you assuming some things?

Student: Like what?

Teacher: Well, for one thing, you're assuming that the factors that affect plant growth are all outside of the plant—water, air, and light. What about anything on the inside of the plant? There's also something else that you're assuming that's important in finding the answer. See if you can discover what it is.

Comparing and Contrasting

Comparison usually involves several skills. Some types of comparisons involve simply making lists of attributes and then delineating the similarities. More sophisticated types of comparisons involve making analogies between seemingly dissimilar objects or phenomena or even using extended metaphors. Contrasts, of course, involve finding differences between objects or events.

Teachers are generally very good at making comparisons since they are required to do so on a daily basis when teaching new concepts to children. Thus, comparing and contrasting can be "modeled" effectively by the teacher's examples. The teacher can then elicit comparisons and contrasts by asking questions such as "What do these things have in common?" "In what ways are these things different?" "Have you ever seen anything like this before?"

EXAMPLE:

Student A: I still can't figure out why the leaves at the top of an oak tree are a different shape than the leaves on the bottom.

Teacher: What other types of objects can you think of in which the only difference between the top and bottom is the shape?

Student B: Tall buildings downtown.

Student C: Yeah, and mountains.

Teacher: Good. That's a start. Now what might an oak tree, a tall building, and a mountain have in common?

LESS FREQUENTLY USED SKILLS

Applying

This skill is most often used in the additional activities where the student is asked to apply a principle or concept from the puzzle to another set of circumstances.

EXAMPLE:

Teacher: In solving the last puzzle we learned that animals defend territories. How can we apply the idea of territory to humans? Do humans have territories? Do we defend them?

Speculating

Speculation in science involves projecting into the past in order to explain a present phenomenon or projecting into the future to deduce the consequences of a present action. Questions such as "How do you suppose such and such came about?" or "What do you suppose would happen if ...?" are examples of promoting this activity. Some people claim today that the ability to envision alternative futures as consequences of our present actions is a fundamental and necessary skill for all humans—as opposed to the old view that speculation is only for the rich and idle.

EXAMPLE:

Teacher: In the last puzzle we learned that leeches are being used today in some operating rooms to control blood flow. This has created a new business of supplying leeches to operating rooms. What might be the ecological consequences of collecting so many leeches?

Extrapolating

To extrapolate means to "infer beyond the strict evidence." For example, a graph may show a "trend." Students would be asked to "project" future trends from the existing data. This type of projection occurs in business situations all the time. Extrapolating may be non-numerical also.

EXAMPLE:

Student: I read that many mammals have territorial behaviors. I guess other mammals also have this behavior.

Teacher: How would you find out if all mammals exhibit this behavior?

Recognizing Fallacies

Aside from violating the "laws" of formal logic—laws of deductive reasoning—students may occasionally use verbal and material fallacies. Verbal fallacies generally involve "tricks" with words that have double meanings. Material fallacies are simply questions of relevance—either leaving out a point that is relevant or using a point that is irrelevant.

EXAMPLES:

1. If germs are bad for you, how can wheat germ be good for you? (verbal fallacy)

2. How can you condemn Pete for stealing when you do it yourself? (material fallacy)

3. The statement that "Slick and Slippery Butter has only fifty calories per pat" leaves out the relevant fact that those fifty calories are all fat. (material fallacy)

Student Worksheets

FACT–QUESTION–HYPOTHESIS WORKSHEET

Puzzle
Problem:

FACTS	QUESTIONS

HYPOTHESES

Libraries Unlimited, Inc. • P.O. Box 3988 • Englewood, CO 80155-3988   *Nature Puzzlers* (Lawrence E. Hillman)

HYPOTHESIS WORKSHEET			
	Facts explained by hypothesis	Facts not explained by hypothesis	Predictions from hypothesis	Accept or Reject? Why ?
Hypothesis #1				Accept ☐ Reject ☐
Hypothesis #2				Accept ☐ Reject ☐
Hypothesis #3				Accept ☐ Reject ☐
Hypothesis #4				Accept ☐ Reject ☐

Libraries Unlimited, Inc. • P.O. Box 3988 • Englewood, CO 80155-3988   *Nature Puzzlers* (Lawrence E. Hillman)

Nature Puzzlers I
Relatively Easy

Jim placed the ladder against the smooth bark of the dead, branchless tree and began his thirty-foot climb. For Jim, this was all in a day's work. Jim is a biologist who studies screech owls. Today, Jim was in for a surprise! He expected to find an owl's nest. All the signs were there: the owl pellets at the bottom of the tree and the "whitewash" of bird droppings covering the ground. But when he reached the owl's nest at the top of the tree, Jim found snakes!

Snakes often raid birds' nests. They like to eat bird eggs. But these were not the kind of snakes that normally eat bird eggs. These snakes were not only too small, they were also naturally blind.

As Jim watched the owl's nest over the next couple of days, he discovered the real surprise! The mother owl brought the snakes to the nest and allowed them to live there unharmed. This activity was really unusual because owls generally eat snakes or feed them to their young. Jim had never seen owls keep live snakes as pets.

Jim wondered if this was just a freak occurrence. He investigated other owl nests in the same area. He found that thirteen out of seventy-five owl nests had these blind snakes in them.

Jim had a hard time trying to explain this strange owl behavior. How would you explain it?

TEACHER'S KEY

Puzzle: "Strange Companions"—Why does an owl keep live snakes in its nest?
Key Cognitive Skills: Hypothesizing, deduction
Key Concepts: Mutualism, animal intelligence, adaptation
Difficulty Level: Relatively Easy
Sources of Information: See references 5, 40, 43, 53, and 67.

Libraries Unlimited, Inc. • P.O. Box 3988 • Englewood, CO 80155-3988   *Nature Puzzlers* (Lawrence E. Hillman)

Background Information and Solution

Scientists who study owls often examine owl pellets. When an owl eats a mouse, a snake, or any other animal, it swallows the bones and fur. Since the owl cannot digest bones and fur, these and other undigested material become glued together in the owl's stomach. Sooner or later the owl rids itself of this pellet by vomiting. This pellet usually lands at the bottom of the owl's nesting tree, making it easy for biologists to find their nests.

The best explanation at the time of this writing appears to be that the snakes are used to rid the nest of unwanted parasites. The owl and its offspring are free of infestation (a terrible problem for most birds), and the snake gets a free meal. Blind snakes are generally underground dwellers and their diet consists mainly of small insects. More research needs to be done, however, in order to better understand this phenomenon.

Alternate Hypotheses

1. The owls are saving the snakes as food for their newly hatched chicks. Although this is not stated explicitly in the puzzle, we assume that the snakes are able to survive for awhile after the chicks are born.

2. The snakes keep the owl's eggs warm when the owl is away from its nest. Snakes are cold blooded and, therefore, would be of little help keeping the chicks warm when the air temperature is cool.

3. The snakes scare other predators that might eat the owl's eggs. This hypothesis might be true. How can it be tested?

SUGGESTED ADDITIONAL ACTIVITIES

1. Symbiosis occurs frequently in the natural world. What other mutual relationships exist between animals? Do any mutual relationships exist between an animal and a plant? Do they exist between two plants? A lichen, for example, is a mutual relationship between a fungus and an algae. The relationship between a remora fish and a shark is a good example of mutualism between two animals. Encourage students to research other examples of mutualism between animals, between plants, and between animals and plants.

2. Do you think that most parasitic relationships result in mutualistic relationships after a long time on an evolutionary scale? For example, maybe the fungus that now lives with the algae to create a lichen was once a parasite on the algae. But, as time went on, the algae adapted to the fungus and used it as a partner in survival. Do you think the owl and snake relationship might have started as parasitism?

3. One of the most difficult things to explain in animal behavior is how specific behaviors begin. Speculate about how this relationship between screech owls and blind snakes might have begun. Why is it so difficult to study the origin of specific behaviors? Will we ever really know how specific behaviors originate in nature? Will we ever know why humans do some of the things we do? Why and how did we start shaking hands, kissing, nodding our heads in place of saying the word "yes"?

4. Why do humans have pets? Was the snake a "pet" for the owl? What similarities and differences do you see between the snake as the owl's pet and a dog as a human's pet? Is the man-dog relationship parasitic or mutualistic?

5. What predictions can you make from the solution to this puzzle? Remember that the answer is only a hypothesis and, therefore, requires further testing. For example, one prediction might be that fewer owls will die from diseases caused by parasites since the snakes are consuming them. How would you test this prediction or others that you have made?

6. Owls are part of a group of birds called raptors. Raptors have muscles in their legs that force the talons in their feet to close tightly around prey when the legs are in certain positions. The screech owl has to be very "careful" when carrying a snake to its nest. Could this be a sign of intelligence in the owl? How would you test an animal's intelligence? What is intelligence? Why do some people say that animals are only machines—creatures of habit instead of intelligent beings?

7. Owl pellets can be obtained from some biological supply houses. Order a quantity for your class. Have the students examine the contents for bones, fur, seeds, and so on. Encourage students to classify the bones by visible structure and attempt to identify the kind of animals to which the bones belong.

Funny Running into You

We had been in the air for only a few minutes when we heard a loud bang coming from the front of the plane. It didn't sound like an explosion. It sounded more like someone hit the side of the jet with a sledgehammer. The captain of our Alaskan Airlines jet announced over the intercom that there was nothing to worry about. The jet had just collided with a fish, but the damage was only minor.

We thought the captain was joking. But when we arrived at our destination, we knew that the pilot had been telling the truth. Part of the fish's back fin was still clinging to the side of the jet's windshield.

I still don't believe it! How can a jet plane collide with a fish?

Libraries Unlimited, Inc. • P.O. Box 3988 • Englewood, CO 80155-3988

Nature Puzzlers (Lawrence E. Hillman)

TEACHER'S KEY

Puzzle: "Funny Running into You"—How can a jet and a fish collide?
Key Cognitive Skills: Strictly a "fun" problem, hypothesizing (brainstorming)
Key Concepts: Accidental human-wildlife interactions
Difficulty Level: Relatively Easy
Sources of Information: See reference 44.

Background Information and Solution

This exercise is fun for brainstorming hypotheses because the situation seems so improbable. However, this situation actually did occur. An Alaskan Airlines jet inadvertently was on the same flight path as a bald eagle that happened to be carrying a large fish. The startled eagle dropped the fish when it swerved to avoid the jet.

Alternate Hypotheses

Students will offer some rather humorous possibilities to explain this phenomenon—swordfish that apparently can jump incredible heights, cargo planes carrying fish that are flying at higher altitudes and one fish falls out, and so forth. Encourage students to offer all of their hypotheses, no matter how unusual they might be. Remember, brainstorming is a non-judgmental activity and even far-fetched ideas are acceptable. In fact, far-fetched examples add a bit of comic relief to the sometimes dry environment of the classroom.

SUGGESTED ADDITIONAL ACTIVITIES

1. Human-wildlife encounters can be serious, humorous, or planned. Have students write a short story about their own encounters with wildlife in the city or countryside.

2. Birds flying into the engines of jet planes is a serious problem. This situation is dangerous for both humans and birds. Brainstorm ways to solve this problem. Consider ways that are both feasible and outrageous. Keep in mind that neither the birds nor the planes can be eliminated. Resist the temptation to be judgmental about any suggestion that arises.

3. Suppose that part of the fish in this puzzle had not remained attached to the jet. How would the pilot prove that he or she was not seeing things? Assume that the other flight engineers or passengers had not seen the fish.

4. Have students use the library media center to find stories about other strange events involving wildlife and humans and report their findings to the class.

5. Ask students to read a less humorous account of wildlife-human interaction in reference 44. Encourage them to write their opinions about this article.

Libraries Unlimited, Inc. • P.O. Box 3988 • Englewood, CO 80155-3988   *Nature Puzzlers* (Lawrence E. Hillman)

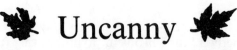 Uncanny

---

Earthquake Hits San Francisco

May 15, 2008

An earthquake registering 7.8 on the Richter scale rocked downtown San Francisco at 4:00 p.m. yesterday. Residents of local highrise buildings scurried down stairwells in an attempt to

"This is unbelievable!" John said as he handed Leo an odd looking piece of scrap paper. "Your new student is right on the money."

"What are you talking about?" asked Leo, the head scientist at the Earthquake Center in Los Angeles.

"Your new student, Janet, has been posting her earthquake predictions on the lunchroom bulletin board. At first I thought it was a joke. But when I compared her predictions for the last five months with the actual data, she was correct nearly every time."

Leo examined the piece of paper. John had written the actual dates and intensities of recent earthquakes next to Janet's predictions. "You're right. These predictions are about 85 percent accurate. How did she do it?" Leo asked.

"That's why I came to you," John said. "I thought maybe the two of you had developed a new method for predicting earthquakes and were keeping it a secret from me."

"Well, somebody is keeping a secret. I'll see what I can find out from Janet," Leo said.

The next day, Leo called Janet into his office. "Janet, I understand that you have developed a new method for predicting earthquakes. Why haven't you told me about it?"

Janet blushed. "It's just that the method isn't very scientific," she said.

"Nonsense," Leo said. "You have an accuracy of 85 percent. It can't be luck."

"Well, it's pretty simple," she said. "If I want to know whether there will be an earthquake tomorrow, I just read today's newspaper!"

"That's ridiculous. How can ...?"

Before Leo could finish his question, Janet turned toward the door, smiled, and said, "You're a brilliant scientist—you figure it out."

TEACHER'S KEY

Puzzle: "Uncanny"—How does a student make earthquake predictions?
Key Cognitive Skills: Deduction, hypothesizing, giving reasons for hypotheses
Key Concepts: Animal senses
Difficulty Level: Moderately Easy
Sources of Information: See references 16 and 21.

Libraries Unlimited, Inc. • P.O. Box 3988 • Englewood, CO 80155-3988   *Nature Puzzlers* (Lawrence E. Hillman)

Background Information and Solution

Solving this problem requires students to search through the newspaper in order to find a section or sections that might have some link to earthquakes. Since the connection is so subtle, students will come up with many hypotheses in their search. This puzzle gives the teacher an opportunity to ask students to give reasons for their hypotheses.

Janet was reading the lost and found columns in the newspaper. Some evidence exists that animals, particularly cats, sense the coming of earthquakes and, as a result, run away or hide. Their owners consequently report them missing. Janet keeps a daily record of missing cats and correlates these statistics with known earthquakes. She then predicts the date and intensity of new earthquakes based on her records.

Alternate Hypotheses

Students might suggest any number of the following correlations: changes in weather patterns, increase in crime, changes in tides, reports of poltergeists, unusual astronomical events, reports of meteorites, increase in accidents—automobile or otherwise, and so forth.

SUGGESTED ADDITIONAL ACTIVITIES

1. Janet claimed that her method was not scientific, but perhaps it was. She discovered a correlation between missing animals and earthquakes, collected statistics to quantify the relationship, and used the data to predict new earthquakes. Is Janet's approach science or pseudoscience? Debate this issue in class.

2. Animals and humans are sometimes said to have a "sixth sense." What exactly does that mean? Discuss experiences that students have had with their "sixth sense" and discuss the basis in science these experiences might have.

3. Cats have remarkably good senses of sight, hearing, and smell. How do a cat's senses differ structurally, physiologically, and functionally from human senses? Is it possible that a cat can pick up sensory data prior to an earthquake that humans cannot perceive? Have students write reports on animal senses that show major differences among the animal kingdom.

4. Changes in weather are often said to bring about biological changes. For example, windy weather may have some effect on human emotions—perhaps causing depression or anxiety. Carry out some statistical experiments (similar to Janet's) to test the effects of weather on human emotions. How would you design such experiments and carry them out? What problems would you face? How certain are the results?

5. What is the range of human differences in sensory perception? Use the class as a representative population to test individual differences in eyesight, hearing, touch, taste, and smell. What causes these differences? Are the differences biological, psychological, or a combination of both? Make graphs (normal curves) showing the range of individual differences in the class. Compare these graphs with other graphs for larger populations. Graphs are found in most introductory psychology texts. Is the class representative of the larger population? What is a representative sample?

Libraries Unlimited, Inc. • P.O. Box 3988 • Englewood, CO 80155-3988   *Nature Puzzlers* (Lawrence E. Hillman)

Look Out Below!

When you look at a clothesline what do you expect to find—clothes, right? Well, not if you're at Joan's house. On her clothesline you are likely to find a sloth. You see, Joan lives in Central America. She is a biologist who studies the habits of tree sloths.

Tree sloths are cuddly creatures about two feet tall, with lots of greenish-colored hair. They live in the jungle. They are called tree sloths because they spend most of their time climbing trees. Their long arms and legs make them good but very slow climbers. A sloth may take as long as 15 minutes to climb a tree! On the ground sloths are even slower, since their arms and legs are not easy to use on level ground.

Joan took a couple of tree sloths home as pets, because they were too difficult to study in the jungle. The green algae that grows in their hair makes them almost impossible to find against the green background of the trees. Sloths can hang motionless for hours in the high branches, so they look just like any other tree branch.

Joan observed the sloth's habits over many months. She watched as they basked in the sun or climbed the woodwork in her house. But she realized something strange about the sloth's behavior. The sloths were naturally housebroken—they never "went to the bathroom." Then one day her favorite sloth, Speedy, got into a bowl of boiled rice and had to be cleaned off. As usual, she hung the sloth on the clothesline by its arms and legs and began to wash Speedy with the hose. As soon as Joan turned the hose on Speedy, he quickly dropped his stored-up fecal material. Joan found this strange behavior also to be true of the other sloths. They would go to the bathroom only when they were hosed down.

How would you explain this strange behavior?

TEACHER'S KEY

Puzzle: "Look Out Below!"—What causes an unusual behavior in tree sloths?
Key Cognitive Skills: Deduction, hypothesizing
Key Concepts: Animal camouflage
Difficulty Level: Relatively Easy
Sources of Information: See references 5 and 21.

Background Information and Solution

The jungle environment is full of predators. Sloths must be careful to conceal their where-abouts at all times. Visual camouflage, of course, is one way to accomplish this task. Sloths have green algae in their hair to make them difficult to see among the trees. Sound may lead a predator to its prey. The sound of falling fecal pellets may signal a predator on the ground and show the pred-ator the location of the sloth. In order to conceal this sound, the sloth defecates only during a rain shower. The sound of the rain covers the sounds of the sloth. A special pouch in the animal's intestine stores the fecal material until the next rain—usually only a day's wait.

Alternate Hypotheses

1. Animals often will defecate when they are scared. The water from the hose scared the sloth and caused it to defecate.

2. The water did not cause the animal to defecate. Instead, hanging the animal upside down forced the animal to defecate.

3. The sloth defecated to mark its territory outside the house.

SUGGESTED ADDITIONAL ACTIVITIES

1. In what other areas of animal life does sound play an important part? Encourage students to do research in the library media center to answer this question. Have students report their findings to the class.

2. Have students try to generalize the solution to this puzzle and turn it into a principle—"All animals disguise sound in order to avoid predators." Discuss the truth of such a principle. Do birds disguise the sound of their baby chicks? How could this be accomplished? How can the principle be modified to make more sense?

3. Ask students to comment on this question: "If you had to survive in the jungle after a plane crash, how would you keep from being found by tigers or leopards?" Encourage students to write their responses in paragraph form.

4. The proposed solution to this puzzle makes sense, but the answer is still not final. How could this hypothesis be further tested? For example, how could Joan see if any loud noise would cause the sloth to defecate? How would you design the experiment? Have students think of ways to test other hypotheses mentioned in class.

5. Speculate—from an evolutionary point of view—how this behavior might have evolved.

6. Joan was allowed to keep the sloths in her home because she was a trained biologist. However, it is illegal in many parts of the world—including the United States—to keep wild animals as pets. Caring for sick or injured wild animals in the home also is illegal. Why do you think these rules exist? What is the reasoning behind these laws?

 # The Cold Facts

Atlanta, November 1930

Scientists reported today some alarming news. The world death rate due to natural causes sky-rocketed last year to nearly unprecedented heights.

Only in 1918 had the death rate reached such extreme proportions. In that year, deaths due to heart attack, pneumonia, kidney failure, and other internal causes increased to ten times the normal rate. A similar, but less dramatic, increase also occurred in 1890.

Although scientists admit to being puzzled by this phenomenon, they are confident a reasonable explanation can be found.

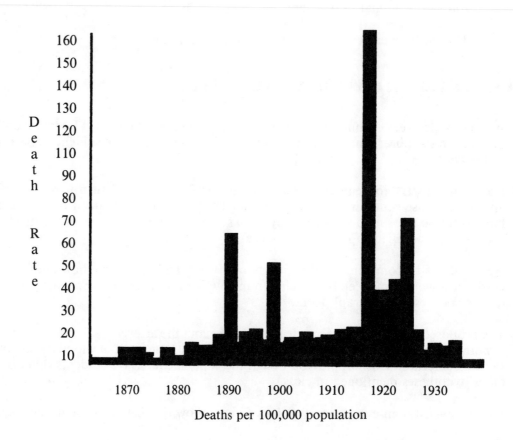

Deaths per 100,000 population

Libraries Unlimited, Inc. • P.O. Box 3988 • Englewood, CO 80155-3988   *Nature Puzzlers* (Lawrence E. Hillman)

TEACHER'S KEY

Puzzle: "The Cold Facts"—What caused a large and unexplained increase in the world death rate?

Key Cognitive Skills: Induction (finding a common cause for multiple effects) fact-finding, hypothesizing

Key Concepts: Disease, epidemics, pandemics, virus, physiological effects of disease

Difficulty Level: Relatively Easy. (The most difficult part of this puzzle is finding the common denominator in the years of increased death rate.)

Sources of Information: See the first suggested additional activity in this section.

Background Information and Solution

Before 1933, little was known about the influenza virus. When people died from complications of influenza, the death certificates would show only the immediate cause of death—heart attack, pneumonia, and so forth. This practice also was due to the fact that doctors did not even suspect their patients had influenza. Since influenza kills many older people and those with chronic lung and heart disease, doctors assumed that heart attack and pneumonia were the actual causes of death.

In the beginning, encourage students to find historical facts about the years in question. This exercise is a good example of learning how to limit a search, recognizing relevant ideas, and utilizing other skills involved in searching for information. Once some fact-finding has been accomplished, brainstorm the hypotheses.

Alternate Hypotheses

1. The increase in deaths was caused by international wars. For some reason, this suggestion is common from students—even though it is easily refuted by the fact that the newspaper article states that the death rate is from "natural causes."

2. The "plague" caused the rise in death rate. This hypothesis is a closer approximation to the solution, but is obviously false.

SUGGESTED ADDITIONAL ACTIVITIES

1. The history of pandemics caused by the influenza virus is a fascinating excursion into "scientific method." Because so many puzzles remain about how the virus spreads, what happens to it in years when there are few or no outbreaks, why some strains suddenly appear that are more virulent than others, the study of its scientific history can provide opportunities for students to make further hypotheses. A good source of information on this topic is *The Natural History of Viruses* by C. H. Andrews, New York: W. W. Norton and Co., 1967.

2. Despite a great deal of research, the common cold still remains unconquered. Many theories (both scientific and not so scientific) have been proposed for preventing the common cold: high potency vitamin C regimens, special diets, exercise regimens, antiseptic mouthwashes, and so forth. Have students research their favorite "preventive medicines" for the cold, report on their findings, and debate the issue in a class forum. This exercise can reinforce many cognitive skills.

Libraries Unlimited, Inc. • P.O. Box 3988 • Englewood, CO 80155-3988   *Nature Puzzlers* (Lawrence E. Hillman)

3. Viruses are said to inhabit the hinterland between the living and nonliving. For example, they can reproduce only when inside a living cell. Viruses lack essential cellular structures such as the nucleus. Some can survive indefinite periods of time under the most hostile of circumstances—some scientists even believe that viruses could survive the lunar environment. Discuss the criteria for calling something a "living thing." Can all things be considered alive in some sense? If not, what is the difference between livng and nonliving?

4. Using the graph on the student handout ask students to extrapolate when they believe the next flu pandemic occurred in history and give reasons for their predictions. Ask students to check their extrapolations with the facts—the next pandemic occurred in 1957. Encourage students to revise extrapolations to make new predictions and give new reasons for their theories.

A Crawling Suit

When I felt the bee move slowly across my lower lip, I froze in fear! The tiny wire cage strapped to the top of my head felt odd.

"Don't make any sudden movements, Marc," Sam said to me. Sam knows about bees. He is an apiarist—a beekeeper.

I tried to be calm as three more bees landed on my bare face. Then, ten more bees landed ... then fifty ... then two hundred. Within a minute, my face and upper body were covered with thousands of honeybees.

Sam took a credit card and carefully removed a few bees from around my eyes. "I'm just making sure your new suit of bees fits nicely," Sam said with a grin.

"Don't do that!" I said. "They're going to sting me!" Every once and awhile I could see a bee's stinger. I had enough bees on me now to kill a horse.

"They aren't going to sting you," Sam said. "When we get a new world's record for the most bees on a person's body, you'll forget about being afraid."

It made me feel a little better to see bees crawling on Sam's bare skin. They weren't stinging him either.

Sam and his helper put me on a scale. After subtracting my body weight, they calculated that the bees weighed twenty-three pounds. This was a new world's record, beating the old record by two pounds!

Sam was right. I didn't get stung. Why was he so sure? Why was that little cage strapped to the top of my head? (P.S.—I found out later that if just one bee had stung me, they all might have stung me. I'm glad I didn't know that at the time!)

TEACHER'S KEY

Puzzle: "A Crawling Suit"—Why doesn't a boy get stung when his body is covered with bees?
Key Cognitive Skills: Fact-finding, hypothesizing, deduction
Key Concepts: Animal communication, pheromones, aggression
Difficulty Level: Relatively Easy (Most students are at least somewhat familiar with bees.)
Sources of Information: See references 7, 14, 26, and 65.

Libraries Unlimited, Inc. • P.O. Box 3988 • Englewood, CO 80155-3988   *Nature Puzzlers* (Lawrence E. Hillman)

Background Information and Solution

This puzzle asks two questions: "Why aren't the bees stinging?" and "How are the bees made to land on the boy's body in the first place?" Solving the problem involves discovering that there is a "mechanics" of stinging and that bees communicate using pheromones—a means of chemical communication. The solution requires students to brainstorm ways of using pheromone communication to attract the bees and also ways to interrupt the mechanics of stinging.

Here is the typical solution: Honeybees are not very aggressive by nature but will attack if provoked. Beekeepers, therefore, feed them large amounts of honey before working with them. The honey fills the bee's abdomen making it difficult for the bee to bend and, therefore, to insert its stinger. The beekeeper attracts the bees to Marc by placing the queen bee in a wire cage on Marc's head. Her scent attracts the drones.

Alternate Hypothesis

1. The bees were specially bred to be nonaggressive. This hypothesis is partially true but does not explain why the bees did not sting when they are "aggravated" by the credit card.

2. Marc's skin was treated with a special chemical that the stingers could not penetrate. Sam had bees crawling on his bare skin and was not stung either. In addition, a chemical that would prevent stingers from penetrating the skin would also be so thick as to be noticeable on Sam. Marc described Sam's skin as "bare."

SUGGESTED ADDITIONAL ACTIVITIES

1. What other types of animals use chemical signals (pheromones) to communicate? Have students use the library media center to investigate answers to this question. Then, ask students to report on chemical signals used by cats, ants, deer, dogs, or other domestic or wild animals.

2. What makes an animal aggressive—including humans? Have a class discussion on the similarities and differences between animal and human aggression. For example, many animals fight to protect a territory from other members of their species. Do humans have territories that they defend?

3. What is the difference between the common European honeybee—the species used in this puzzle—and the South American (originally African) variety commonly called "killer bees"? Why are the killer bees more aggressive? When killer bees are genetically crossed with less aggressive varieties, the offspring are aggressive. What does this result tell you about aggressiveness as a genetic trait? Is it a dominant trait? If so, why is it an advantageous trait for bees? If it were advantageous, why did the European bee evolve to be less aggressive? Speculate on possible answers to these questions.

4. If a bee stings another insect, the bee will not necessarily die. However, if it stings a human or other mammal, it will die. What might be the reason for this occurrence? The answer is that the flesh of a soft skinned animal, such as a human, tightly grips the stinger's barbs, making it impossible for the bee to leave the scene without giving up the loosely attached stinger and some of the abdomen. The eviscerated bee eventually dies. The bee will not necessarily lose its stinger to an insect with an exoskeleton because many exoskeletons do not grip the stinger's barbs.

5. Some people seem to be stung by bees more often than others. Is this situation just bad luck? What might be other causes of bee stings? Do color of clothes or perfume scents have anything to do with bee attacks? Encourage students to suggest experiments that might help differentiate some of the factors that cause bee stings.

Scalpel, Suture, Leech

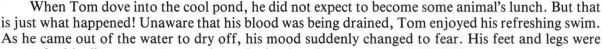

When Tom dove into the cool pond, he did not expect to become some animal's lunch. But that is just what happened! Unaware that his blood was being drained, Tom enjoyed his refreshing swim. As he came out of the water to dry off, his mood suddenly changed to fear. His feet and legs were covered with slimy worms—or at least that's what they looked like. Each black lump of slime throbbed as it took another sip of Tom's blood. Some were tiny blobs, the size of a dime. Others were long and thin like noodles. Two tiny round suckers—one at each end—held each blob in place until it drank its fill of blood.

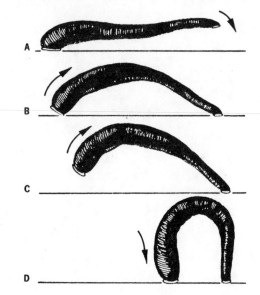

Tom pulled off as many of the bloodsuckers as he could. The rest just fell off when they finished their tasty meal. Tom's blood took a long time to stop flowing from the wounds—like when you cut yourself with paper or a sharp knife. This scared Tom and he ran for help.

As you probably know, Tom was not in any danger. The slimy blobs were leeches. The leech (a relative of the earthworm) is a parasite that feeds on the blood of certain animals. The three small cutting teeth in the suckers of the leeches do not cause serious injury. Tom's blood just took longer than normal to clot.

During the eighteenth and nineteenth centuries, leeches were used by doctors to cure many diseases. People believed that the leech drained out "bad blood." Of course, modern doctors do not use leeches to cure illness—or do they?

Actually, modern medicine is looking again at the leech as a help in curing certain diseases. Some surgeons use them in modern operating rooms. What medical value could these creatures possibly have?

TEACHER'S KEY

Puzzle: "Scalpel, Suture, Leech ..."—How are leeches used in modern operating rooms?
Key Cognitive Skills: Applying, deduction
Key Concepts: Circulatory system, blood
Difficulty Level: Relatively Easy
Sources of Information: See references 35 (for the first suggested additional activity) and 53.

Libraries Unlimited, Inc. • P.O. Box 3988 • Englewood, CO 80155-3988   *Nature Puzzlers* (Lawrence E. Hillman)

Background Information and Solution

The key to solving this problem is understanding the survival problems of leeches. The leech must do more than simply slice into the victim's skin and drink the blood. After all, blood tends to clot. Therefore, the leech must inject a chemical into the victim's tissues to reduce clotting. This substance is called hirudin. Furthermore, a rapid blood flow from the victim is highly desirable. The leech injects chemicals (by way of its saliva) that break down the cohesion between cells and dilate blood vessels to this purpose. Finally, leeches do not eat frequently. Some may go as long as a year between feedings. An antibiotic inside the leech prevents undigested blood from decomposing for as long as six months.

The medical uses of these chemicals include the prevention of blood clots and the treatment of rheumatism and contusions. The chemical that breaks down the cohesion of cells (hyaluronidase) can be used to increase the absorption of injected drugs or anesthetics. The antibiotic in the leech's gut may have important applications for the control of some diseases.

Alternate Hypotheses

1. Leeches are used to drain blood temporarily from certain tissues in order to control bleeding during an operation.

2. Leeches are used to detect harmful microorganisims in the patients blood. If the leeches die, the patient has a harmful disease.

SUGGESTED ADDITIONAL ACTIVITIES

1. What are some commonly known and used natural or home remedies? Which of these remedies have become part of modern medicine? What medicines today still come from natural sources? Have students research these topics and report their findings to the class. See, for example, reference 35.

2. The use of leeches in medical research and clinics has stimulated a new "industry"—the collection of leeches for sale to laboratories. This collection has caused concern among environmentalists about reducing the populations of leeches in the wild. What is the ecological significance of leeches? How do leeches help to maintain the "balance of nature"? How can the problem of removing leeches from the environment be solved?

3. What are the ethical questions involved in using leeches in this type of scientific research? Discuss with students the pros and cons of this question. You may want to have interested students form two teams to debate this issue.

Making a Break

When I lived in a house with a big backyard, I used to wonder why every so often a bird would fly into one of our windows. My neighbor said that birds see the reflection of the sky in the window pane and fly toward it. So, I paid a lot of money to have my windows tilted slightly downward so that the sky did not reflect in them. Guess what? It didn't work. Birds kept crashing through the windows. I wonder if anybody can come up with a less costly solution.

TEACHER'S KEY

Puzzle: "Making a Break" — Why do birds keep flying through a man's window panes?
Key Cognitive Skills: Observing, applying
Key Concepts: Animal defences
Difficulty Level: Relatively Easy
Sources of Information: See references 16, 21 (for the first suggested additional activity), and 40.

Background Information and Solution

The main point of this puzzle is to encourage students to observe carefully and then apply their observations to a practical situation. Have students observe birds on the ground, particularly ones feeding in groups. Ask them to watch carefully how birds make their escape when threatened by a predator or human. Students, in most cases, will observe at least two things: the birds scatter in a circular pattern in many directions and they fly very low to the ground as they take off. Once these observations are made, ask students to attempt an explanation for what they observe. The reasons are fairly simple. The scattering causes some confusion in the predator; the low take-off angle makes for quicker acceleration.

Now students are faced with the difficult part of this puzzle — trying to figure out a way to keep the low-flying birds from crashing into a window. The possible solutions are often very creative. For example, some people have put life-like drawings of hawks, falcons, owls, and other predatory birds on their window panes to make the low-flying birds veer away. Encourage students to come up with even better solutions.

SUGGESTED ADDITIONAL ACTIVITIES

1. Not all animals scatter when attacked by predators. For example, the musk ox of Alaska form a closely packed ring with their heads facing outward in all directions. Some animals, such as elephants, charge their attackers. Encourage students to use the library media center to research some of the ways different species of animals respond to an attack as a group. Have students hypothesize about the differences. Is the size of the animal significant? Is the size of the herd a factor?

2. How do individual humans behave in a group when threatened physically? Read descriptions provided by plane crash survivors or hijack victims about the behavior of people in crisis situations. Search magazines for articles describing such events. Encourage students to compare the described behaviors and develop some general principles.

3. Birds can be frightened easily by planes—but not all the time. What factors might determine the birds' reactions to planes? (Hint: What would remind the birds of a predator?) Read a short description of Tinbergen and Lorenz's experiment with cut-out predator shapes. Have students critique the experiment in terms of how convincing it is. (See, for example, Tinbergen, N. "Social Releasers and the Experimental Method Required for Their Study." *Wilson Bulletin* 60:6-51 or Tinbergen, N. *The Study of Instinct*. Fair Lawn, N.J.: Oxford University Press, 1951.)

Questions, Questions, Questions

Some of the most ordinary things in life can be puzzling. Can you answer these questions?

1. Why do cats rub against a person's legs?

2. Why does the hair on a person's arms become thinner toward the shoulder?

3. Why don't dogs have sweat glands?

4. Why do coconuts have milk?

5. Where does dust come from?

6. Why don't evergreen trees lose their leaves in the winter?

7. Why are waterfalls white if water is clear?

8. Why do I sometimes see spots before my eyes or hear ringing in my ears?

9. Why do cats fight so much?

10. Why do some kinds of music sound better than others?

Maybe none of the above questions interest you. If not, ask a question about something ordinary that you have always wondered about. Then, try to find the answer!

TEACHER'S KEY

Puzzle: "Questions, Questions, Questions"—When does something ordinary become something puzzling?
Key Cognitive Skills: Questioning, fact-finding
Key Concepts: Varies with questions
Difficulty Level: Relatively Easy
Sources of Information: Any of the sources listed in the bibliography may help with this puzzler.

Background Information and Solution

The whole point of this activity is to reinforce the skill of questioning. Students are engaged in creating their own "puzzler" and then attempting to answer it. When students have selected their own personal question to be answered, have them make a list of additional questions that will guide them in their search for an answer. For example, if a student is thoroughly engaged by the question "Why do coconuts have milk?" then have him or her produce additional questions such as, "What kind of plant produces coconuts?" "What part of the plant is a coconut?" "Is a coconut a seed or a fruit?" and so forth—the more questions the better.

The teacher may notice a similarity between this exercise and certain reading techniques that involve questioning. This similarity is not accidental. The ability to ask questions—lots of questions—is the "soul" of both inquiry and critical reading. Therefore, the teacher should emphasize that the quality, variety, and number of questions in this exercise are more important than eventually finding the answers.

SUGGESTED ADDITIONAL ACTIVITIES

1. Have students present their personal "puzzler" to the class. Ask other students to guess what types of questions were asked to find the answer. Encourage students to offer suggestions for additional questions that could have been asked but were not.

2. The type of question one asks often determines the type of answer one receives. Write the following questions on the chalkboard and then discuss how one might find the answers to them (including other questions that need to be asked). Encourage students to use the library media center to research the answer to at least one question.

   a. What is a halcyon?

   b. What is the meaning of life?

   c. How do you ride a bicycle?

   d. Who discovered America?

   e. How do we know that everything is made of atoms?

   f. What do we mean when we say something is valuable?

   g. How can I make myself a better person?

   h. Why does the moon glow?

   i. Why does the universe exist?

   j. Who was Roy Rogers?

   k. Who am I?

3. Make an attempt to place the above questions into the following categories: questions about facts, questions about meaning of terms, questions about value, questions about processes, and questions demanding explanations. Discuss what processes are used to answer these different types of questions.

Libraries Unlimited, Inc. • P.O. Box 3988 • Englewood, CO 80155-3988   *Nature Puzzlers* (Lawrence E. Hillman)

Which one of the insects or arachnids shown on this page is the most dangerous to humans?

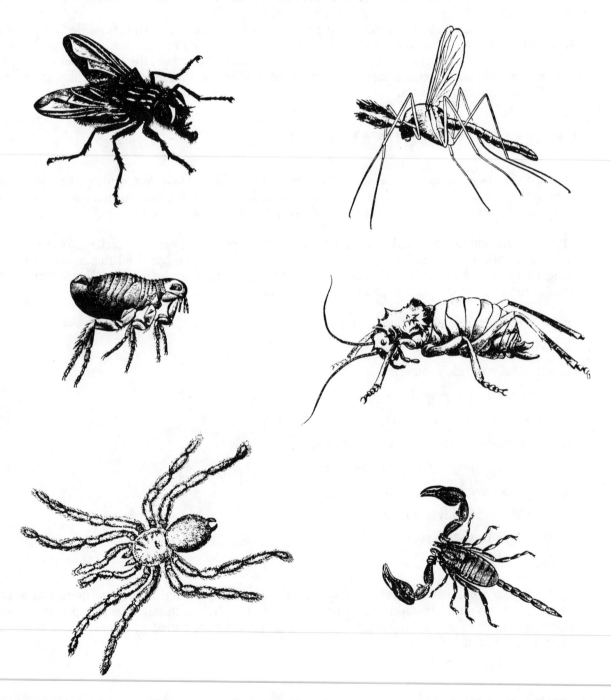

Libraries Unlimited, Inc. • P.O. Box 3988 • Englewood, CO 80155-3988   *Nature Puzzlers* (Lawrence E. Hillman)

TEACHER'S KEY

Puzzle: "Most Dangerous Game" — What is the most dangerous insect or arachnid to humans?
Key Cognitive Skills: Defining, fact-finding
Key Concepts: Disease vector
Difficulty Level: Relatively Easy
Sources of Information: See reference 6.

Background Information and Solution

Begin this puzzler with an exercise in definition. Ask students to set criteria for the term "dangerous to humans." Note the wording here — the definition does not pertain to an individual human, but to humans as a group, or species.

Once criteria have been set, have students debate their opinions as to the most dangerous insect or arachnid. Ask students to give as many reasons for their opinions as possible. Then have students research the data on mortality in the library. Students will discover some misconceptions they have about tarantulas and scorpions — not to mention the fact that the most innocent looking of the bunch, the housefly, is the most deadly. It carries thirty-some diseases that are deadly to humans.

The teacher should restrict the possible selections of insects to the ones shown in the illustration.

SUGGESTED ADDITIONAL ACTIVITIES

1. Have students research the following diseases and identify the vectors (agents that transmit the disease) and reservoirs (animals that harbor the disease but do not necessarily transmit it) for each one: rabies, malaria, equine encephalitis, measles, mononucleosis, salmonellosis, plague, tularemia, infectious hepatitis, histoplasmosis, and trichinosis.

2. Ask students to formulate hypotheses to explain the following phenomenon: When a person contracts measles, he or she is immune for life. However, people can catch colds many times.

3. Is the only good bacterium a dead bacterium? With the plethora of antiseptics available on the market today, one would imagine that humans think so. Have students read about bacteria that are beneficial to humans. Examples of beneficial bacteria include bacteria used in making cheese, bacteria in the human intestinal tract, bacteria that clean up sewage, bacteria on our skin, and so forth. See reference 35 for more information.

4. Have students collect advertising for antiseptic products — labels from bottles or cans, television advertisements, and so forth. Critique these advertisements on the basis of their loosely defined terms (or doublespeak), relevancy of statements or commercial content, assumptions, clarity of message, and technique or form of message. After some discussion, have students write a short essay on "How Not to be Fooled by the Media."

A Tale of Twin Cities

Jonestown and Smithsville are two towns in the southwestern part of the United States. They are merely ten miles apart and were built to be "twin" cities. Jonestown is just west of Smithsville. The two cities are identical in size, with nearly identical buildings. They share an industrial center between them. Why are the average temperatures of Smithsville consistently lower throughout the year than those of Jonestown?

Month	Average Temperature of Jonesville	Average Temperature of Smithsville
May	50 degrees	45 degrees
June	61 degrees	54 degrees
July	80 degrees	75 degrees
August	85 degrees	79 degrees

TEACHER'S KEY

Puzzle: "Tale of Twin Cities"—Why does one city have lower temperatures than the other?
Key Cognitive Skills: Fact-finding, applying
Key Concepts: Relationship between albedo and atmospheric temperature
Difficulty Level: Relatively Easy
Sources of Information: See references 13, 20, 39, and 50.

Background Information and Solution

In order to solve this puzzle, students will first need to collect information (either through discussion or library research) on factors that affect temperature—color of objects, reflection, absorption, heat capacity, and so forth. After students have collected the necessary information, ask them to apply these principles to make guesses about the difference between the two cities. The major difference is that Smithsville has more vegetation. The sun's energy is used up partly in evaporating water from the plants and thus cooling temperatures.

Alternate Hypotheses

1. The color of the buildings in Jonestown is darker than in Smithsville, so the city absorbs more sunlight and reflects more infrared radiation. This hypothesis is refuted by the facts in the puzzle.

2. Smithsville has more clouds caused by pollution because it is downwind from the industrial complex. The clouds cool the temperature. This hypothesis is good, but generally unlikely due to the fact that clouds do not usually form within five miles.

SUGGESTED ADDITIONAL ACTIVITIES

1. The so-called "greenhouse effect"—a general warming trend in the earth's atmosphere—has made the news quite a few times in the past decade. Collect magazine and newspaper articles on this topic and examine the several theories that have emerged to explain it. How do the theories explain the facts and predict the trends? If science is about the "truth," why do so many different opinions exist among scientists about this phenomenon? See reference 20 for more information.

2. What would happen if the average temperature of the earth were to rise just four degrees Fahrenheit? Have students research this question and write stories about how things would change on earth as a result. For example, some scientists believe that the polar ice caps would melt raising the sea level. Cities near the coasts would then be under water. Where would people living in these cities go? How would other cities be able to deal with the new unemployment? What about agriculture that is lost? How would we make up the food deficit?

3. Another theory that has made headlines over recent years is the "nuclear winter" theory. Have students collect articles about this theory and debate the topic, taking the sides of various theorists on the subject. See references 39 and 50 for more information.

Libraries Unlimited, Inc. • P.O. Box 3988 • Englewood, CO 80155-3988 *Nature Puzzlers* (Lawrence E. Hillman)

Stalking

Wildlife photography is not an easy job—particularly when you are new at it. Last week I received an assignment from a nature magazine to photograph beavers in the wilds of Colorado.

Today I spent most of my time wading around in a pond trying to get a good shot of a beaver feeding by the west riverbank. You see, beavers spend much time in the water, but they usually eat the bark of aspen or willow trees that grow by the shore. So I waited ... and waited ... and waited ....

Anyway, the end result of my wait at the pond was a cold chill and an empty roll of film. I could not understand what happened! The day before, I saw a beaver on the same west riverbank and it stayed there for a long time. Naturally I didn't have my camera! Since beavers have to eat often and there was still plenty of food, it should have been there today.

Discouraged, I hiked back to the campground where I was staying. One of the rangers patrolling the campground stopped to chat. I told her of my troubles photographing the beavers. She told me that beavers do not always feed in the same place each day. However, the ranger told me of a very easy way to know where the beaver would be feeding from day to day.

The answer was so obvious that it was hard to believe I didn't think of it. I would tell you, but I hate to give away trade secrets.

TEACHER'S KEY

Puzzle: "Stalking"—How do you find a beaver that seems to be unpredictable?
Key Cognitive Skills: Hypothesizing
Key Concepts: Animal senses, defenses
Difficulty Level: Relatively Easy
Sources of Information: See references 9, 16, 21, and 43.

Libraries Unlimited, Inc. • P.O. Box 3988 • Englewood, CO 80155-3988   *Nature Puzzlers* (Lawrence E. Hillman)

Background Information and Solution

The major factor (except for total lack of food plants) that determines where the beaver feeds is wind. The wind is a source of information about possible predators in the area. The predator's scent is carried by the smallest breeze. Since the majority of the beaver's enemies are land dwellers, the most advantageous place for the beaver to feed is the part of the shore where the wind is blowing from the direction of land to water (often the west bank, but not always). When the beaver picks up the scent of a land predator it can scramble safely into the water.

Alternate Hypotheses

1. Beavers never feed in the same place twice so they will not be discovered by predators trying to learn their routines.

2. Beavers always eat on the part of the shore containing the most vegetation.

3. Other animals feed at the pond as well. The beaver feeds away from ducks, geese, and other animals.

SUGGESTED ADDITIONAL ACTIVITIES

1. Have students conduct library research on how animals sense the presence of predators or prey. What mode of sensing determines the feeding habits of predator or prey? Is the mode dominant? For example, do animals that depend largely on hearing feed mostly at night?

2. Debate this statement: "The feeding habits of herbivores are largely determined by the structure of their sense organs."

3. The wildlife photographer in this story learned something about the eating habits of beavers. What other types of information about beavers would help this wildlife photographer take better pictures of beavers?

4. If a wildlife photographer lives in your area, invite him or her to speak to your class about the habits of animals in the wild. Perhaps the National Park Service, the Division of Wildlife, or a conservation group in your area can recommend someone for this purpose. Have students prepare questions to ask the photographer before he or she arrives in class.

5. Wildlife photographers are often good trackers. A good tracker can obtain a considerable amount of information from a set of animal tracks. Possible types of information include the species of animal, its direction, how fast it was traveling, its sex, its age, and maybe even its general health. What types of signs might one look for in a track to determine these things? Have students suggest experiments that might provide information about the tracks of particular animals. Experiment with human tracks in sand or mud. Have students try to guess the age, sex, height, and weight of an unknown person from his or her track. These are wonderful exercises in observation and logical deduction. It's also lots of fun. (See Puzzler "Off the Beaten Track," on p. 140, for additional activities in tracking.)

🍁 A Growing Problem 🍁

Which animal shown on this page might be the most helpful to scientists in studying cancer?

Libraries Unlimited, Inc. • P.O. Box 3988 • Englewood, CO 80155-3988

Nature Puzzlers (Lawrence E. Hillman)

TEACHER'S KEY

Puzzle: "A Growing Problem"—Which wild animal best helps our understanding of cancer?
Key Cognitive Skills: Comparing and contrasting, fact-finding
Key Concepts: Cell growth
Difficulty Level: Relatively Easy
Sources of Information: "Cancer: The New Synthesis" in *Science 84*, vol. 5, no. 7, 28-39.

Background Information and Solution

The teacher may approach this problem with a very open-ended format. A simple question, such as "How would you go about solving this problem?" ordinarily is sufficient. The objective is to begin students thinking about organizing their inquiries. Students will begin to recognize that in order to solve this problem, they need to find the characteristics of cancerous growth. They must then connect these characteristics with the characteristics of the animals. Students usually assume that the animals are used for drug experimentation when, in fact, a specific characteristic of the animal itself is of interest. The specific characteristic is rapid growth of cells. This characteristic is best exemplified in the horns of the deer which grow very rapidly during the summer prior to rutting.

Alternate Hypotheses

Six possible choices exist along with a variety of reasons for naming any animal in the pictures. Refrain from giving students any answers to their questions. Simply ask them to justify their reasons as best they can. Toward the end of the lesson, ask for a vote of the correct animal based on the best reasons given.

SUGGESTED ADDITIONAL ACTIVITIES

1. Students often have strong feelings one way or another about using animals in scientific research. This reaction provides a good opportunity to have students write an essay taking sides on this issue. The essay can include assumptions they make, reasons for the assumptions, reasons for their opinions, facts to support their beliefs, and so forth. In other words, the essay can be as complex as the situation permits.

2. Many people believe that wild animals should be preserved if for no other reason than some human use might be found for them at some time. Debate this controversial idea.

3. Have students use the library media center to investigate (perhaps in groups) some of the following topics: regeneration, immune system, cell differentiation, toxic chemicals, radiation and radioactive waste, and cell mutation. Ask students to present the information on each topic to the class. Then ask students (in groups) to present a proposal for researching cancer that would be the most efficient and least costly. Debate the proposals.

🍁 The Long Haul 🍁

Sometimes things just do not make sense. The other day I was reading a book that said most birds in North America migrate from north to south. The next paragraph said that most birds in Europe migrate from east to west. Both of those continents are in the northern hemisphere. Why wouldn't the birds in Europe go south for the winter, too?

TEACHER'S KEY

Puzzle: "The Long Haul"—What are the differences between European and North American bird migrations?
Key Cognitive Skills: Map reading, fact-finding
Key Concepts: Geographical barriers, migratory behavior in birds
Difficulty Level: Relatively Easy
Sources of Information: See references 40, 52, and 60.

Background Information and solution

The best way to solve this puzzle is to examine a map of the world. Encourage students to note carefully the major differences between the Old World and New World land masses and features. This study will take some time, but eventually students will begin to see that the southern land masses (wintering quarters for migratory birds) in the Old World are displaced to the west, whereas southern land masses in the New World run nearly north and south. Furthermore, mountain ranges and deserts (barriers to migration) in the Old World run east and west; in the New World these barriers run north and south.

Alternate Hypotheses

1. Birds use star patterns to guide them in their migration. The star patterns are different on these two continents. This argument is fallacious because the star patterns in the Northern Hemisphere are the same for both continents.

Libraries Unlimited, Inc. • P.O. Box 3988 • Englewood, CO 80155-3988   *Nature Puzzlers* (Lawrence E. Hillman)

2. Weather patterns are different in Europe than in North America. These differences change the direction of migration. This hypothesis is better because weather is a factor in migration. However, a climatic map of the two continents shows few differences that would affect migration.

SUGGESTED ADDITIONAL ACTIVITIES

1. The homing instinct of some animals is remarkable. This instinct is not only displayed by migratory animals, but also by domestic animals such as cats and dogs that reportedly travel great distances over unfamiliar terrain to return home. Discuss some of the following theories about homing: using the stars as guides, magnetic field of the earth, guideposts on the ground, and sense of smell. Have students write convincing stories about the "homing" instinct of a domestic animal—either a true story or one that is fictional. Encourage the students to read their stories to the class. Then have classmates decide whether they think the story is true based on how convincing the writer was in developing the "method" by which the animal returned home.

2. Encourage students to develop tests to determine the validity of the following two theories:

   a. Homing pigeons navigate by using the sun and stars as guides.

   b. Homing pigeons navigate by orienting themselves to the earth's magnetic field.

3. Investigate the science of orienteering. Have students write a short story about a child who becomes lost in the woods and finds the way out to safety.

4. What kind of adaptations would a bird need to fly thousands of miles to its summer habitat? Have students "design" an ideal migratory bird, taking into account things such as wing size (big enough for gliding but not too much extra weight), wing shape, body fat, and so forth.

Libraries Unlimited, Inc. • P.O. Box 3988 • Englewood, CO 80155-3988   *Nature Puzzlers* (Lawrence E. Hillman)

Best Friend

Which dog in the pictures below would be the most loyal to its master? Would any other species of dogs be more loyal than the ones shown here?

TEACHER'S KEY

Puzzle: "Best Friend"—What kind of dog would be most loyal to its master?
Key Cognitive Skills: Fact-finding, deduction, defining
Key Concepts: Animal sociology, behavioral genetics
Difficulty Level: Relatively Easy
Sources of Information: See references 22, 61, and 63.

Background Information and Solution

Begin the discussion of this puzzle by having students determine criteria for "loyalty." Will a loyal dog follow only one master or anybody that happens to be holding its lead? Is the most loyal dog always obedient—even to other people? The answers that students give to questions such as these will determine partially the outcome of this investigation.

The key to investigating this puzzle is the recognition that a dog's loyalty to its master is related to its ancestry—particularly its wild ancestry. Dogs descended from the North American wolf are more likely to be loyal to their masters than dogs descended from European ancestry. The reason for this derives from the fact that North American wolves are social animals—they hunt in packs, show extreme loyalty to members of the pack, have a social hierarchy, and exhibit loyalty to a leader. Dogs, such as the husky, become strongly attached to a human early in life. Although these dogs are somewhat independent in their actions, they obey only one master. European dogs, on the other hand, are often descended from the jackal which is a more solitary hunter. Although these dogs are very obedient, they are obedient to nearly anyone who happens by.

With the above information in mind, the teacher may want to guide students through an exercise on fact-finding, concentrating on the ancestry of these dogs and their social relations. When this exercise has been accomplished to everyone's satisfaction, deduce the behavioral consequences from the known facts.

Alternate Hypotheses

Students generally try to solve this problem by giving examples from their personal experiences—particularly concentrating on stories about their own pets. This provides the teacher with the opportunity to direct students' attention toward criteria necessary to define the concept of "loyalty." Remind students that a good hypothesis is not simply a generalization of experience. It must attempt to explain the phenomenon in question. In this case, a partial explanation (see "Suggested Additional Activities" for a problem concerning "genetic fallacy") comes from understanding the origin of a behavior.

SUGGESTED ADDITIONAL ACTIVITIES

1. The belief that a particular phenomenon has been completely explained by its origin is known as the "genetic fallacy." For example, the human handshake is thought to have originated in food passing among higher primates as a gesture of peace or "friendliness." To believe that this hypothesis completely explains the human handshake would be to commit the genetic fallacy.

In part, we have asked students to commit this fallacy in solving the puzzler. To correct this situation, ask students to look for other determinants of dog loyalty that are not genetic—such as the personality of the master, the age it was weaned from its mother, and so forth.

2. Why would anyone bother to study the sociology of dogs, elk, or gorillas? How can information about animal groups be applied to understanding human groups? Discuss these questions with the class. Then have students read some of the suggested literature and return to this question again. See suggested references in the "Teacher Key."

3. How much of human behavior is "determined" by the groups to which we belong? Have students watch a short film (about five minutes) that involves human interaction. Ask students to observe the behavior of the people in the film and write down as many behaviors (including speech) as they can. Then as a class, attempt to categorize these behaviors as individualistic or determined by society. Interestingly, students will often ignore behaviors that are extremely routine or habitual. If this response occurs, point out the conventionality of such behaviors (for example, facing to the front of the elevator).

4. What behaviors in animals are "stereotyped" and which are not? Many examples can be gleaned from pets—the cat "pawing" the furniture, the dog turning in circles before laying down, and the canary singing the same tune as its wild counterparts. Have students make a list of such stereotyped behaviors in a variety of animals. Then encourage students to choose one animal and write a "speculation" on the origins of one or more stereotyped behaviors—for example, "Why My Dog Chases Cars."

Libraries Unlimited, Inc. • P.O. Box 3988 • Englewood, CO 80155-3988   *Nature Puzzlers* (Lawrence E. Hillman)

Web of Reason

Any number of times I have walked along a trail in the woods only to run into a spider's web. Sometimes it is just a single strand of silk run between two trees. One day it occurred to me that this cannot be an easy thing for a spider to do. I mean, how does it tie a single strand of silk between two trees that are sometimes twenty feet apart?

Then one day I saw how one spider did it. It was not what I expected!

Libraries Unlimited, Inc. • P.O. Box 3988 • Englewood, CO 80155-3988

Nature Puzzlers (Lawrence E. Hillman)

TEACHER'S KEY

Puzzle: "Web of Reason"—How does a spider tie a single strand of silk from one tree to another?
Key Cognitive Skills: Hypothesizing, deduction
Key Concepts: Animal locomotion
Difficulty Level: Relatively Easy
Sources of Information: See references 16, 21, and 32 (for the fifth suggested additional activity).

Background Information and Solution

Students can come up with an extraordinary number of hypotheses for this puzzler. The point of the puzzle is to encourage students to draw consequences from their hypotheses. For example, if the student suggests that the spider simply walks down one tree and climbs up the other trailing its silk strand, then a consequence of this hypothesis would be a rather slack piece of silk hanging between the trees.

The answer is somewhat unusual. The spider can "fly" by sending out a strand of silk that will carry it on the wind. This phenomenon is known as ballooning. The spider can also send out a long filament in hopes that a breeze will connect it to a nearby tree. Sometimes students will come up with the answer almost immediately. Do not admit the answer to students too soon. Force students to draw consequences from their ideas and think about their solutions.

This puzzle can, of course, be approached in other ways—as can all the puzzles in this book. One alternative would be to take a "twenty questions" approach to eliminate hypotheses.

Alternate Hypotheses

1. The spider has its mate carry the other end of the silk to the nearby tree. This hypothesis begs the question.

2. The spider jumps to the other tree. This spider would be remarkable indeed!

SUGGESTED ADDITIONAL ACTIVITIES

1. In 1883, the island of Krakatoa literally blew up. The volcano on the island erupted destroying nearly all life on the island. Yet within a short period of time after the lava had cooled, plants were growing, animals (including birds, spiders, and insects) were occupying new niches on the island, and, on the whole, things seemed to be returning to normal. But many of the species were new to the island. How did they get there? Have students hypothesize about the travel methods of these plants and animals.

2. Have students compile a "Book of Records" for speed in the animal world—the fastest bird, the fastest mammal, the fastest fish, and so forth. How have these animals been "designed" for speed as compared to their slower counterparts? What general conclusions can be drawn about design for speed? See references 16 and 21.

Libraries Unlimited, Inc. • P.O. Box 3988 • Englewood, CO 80155-3988   *Nature Puzzlers* (Lawrence E. Hillman)

3. Have students compare the fastest birds in the world with the fastest jets. What similarities do they show? How can the obvious differences in design be explained?

4. Why can some birds glide for long distances while others cannot. Have students compare and contrast gliding birds (such as the albatross and hawk) with nongliding birds (such as the starling and swift). Have students hypothesize about the general principals involved.

5. Ask students to read reference 32. This article deals with the question of efficient locomotive adaptation. Namely, it asks the question "Why don't animals have wheels?" Discuss this article with your students.

It Came from Beyond the Stars

What do you think a visitor from outer space would look like? Like ET? Would it be a robot? How many heads would it have? Actually, the most likely visitor from outer space would look very much like something that already lives here on earth. What living thing on earth do you think probably looks most like earth's first alien visitor?

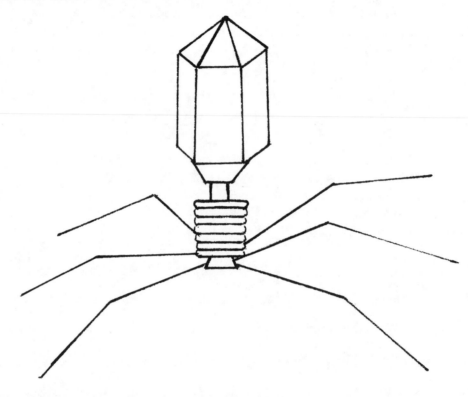

TEACHER'S KEY

Puzzle: "It Came from Beyond the Stars" — What living thing on earth probably looks most like the earth's first alien visitor?

Key Cognitive Skills: Assuming, applying, deduction, defining (in the first suggested additional activity)

Key Concepts: Requirements of life in space

Difficulty Level: Relatively Easy

Sources of Information: See references 1, 9, 16, 18, 21, 25, 33, 40, and 47.

Background Information and Solution

Notice that the puzzle asks for the "most likely" candidate for an alien visitor. In order to solve this puzzle, students must do two things: they must list the requirements for space travel that must be met by any living thing, and they must apply these requirements to various groups of organisms to find the best match.

Requirements for space travel include the following:

1. The ability to remain dormant for long periods of time—thousands, perhaps hundreds of thousands, of years.

2. The ability to subsist on a minimal amount of food or the ability to create its own food.

3. The ability to withstand harsh, inhospitable atmospheres if encountered.

4. The ability to withstand intense cold and/or heat.

Students usually assume that the organism must be some form of humanoid. They often argue that intelligence would be a major criteria for adaptation to space—since fantastic space vehicles would need to be built to carry the required environments and advanced technology to meet the requirements of dormancy, such as suspended animation. This belief is the mythology of the technological age. Point out that many organisms on earth already live in incredibly inhospitable environments. For instance, many mammals and reptiles hibernate for long periods of time without food or water.

One approach to solving the puzzle involves listing animals under each requirement for space travel and then comparing the lists to see which animals satisfy the most criteria. In general, these lists tend to include mostly large animals (bears, sea lions, and so forth). When students are reminded of their assumptions based on their television experiences, they are often quick to recognize small plants and animals—even microscopic ones—as prospects. When this recognition occurs, have students research information on bacteria, algae, and viruses in order to ascertain the organism's living requirements. Students soon learn that the most likely candidate is a virus.

Alternate Hypotheses

1. The aliens are similar to reptiles.

2. The aliens are part plant and part animal. They make their own food by the process of photosynthesis but they can move around on legs similar to animals.

SUGGESTED ADDITIONAL ACTIVITIES

1. Are viruses very primitive organisms (ancient on an evolutionary scale) or are they highly advanced organisms of recent origin? Have students set criteria for making distinctions between what we call "primitive" and "advanced" organisms. Are these criteria arbitrary? Are they based on assumptions about life and its history?

2. Suppose that we could never (ever!) find viruses in the fossil record. This fact could be interpreted in several ways. On one hand, someone could claim that viruses cannot be found in

ancient strata simply because they did not exist in ancient times. On the other hand, someone else could claim that viruses existed in ancient times but could not form fossils due to their structure (no bones to preserve, for example). How can this controversy be resolved? Could any absolute evidence ever exist that would be convincing one way or the other?

3. Have students design a "natural" space station. Everything—food, water, electricity for power, and so forth—would have to be produced by natural means. First, have students set criteria for what is "natural." For example, is nuclear power "natural" if it comes from uranium? These criteria then will set the "rules" for designing the space station. Encourage students to use the library media center to research natural sources of food, water, and so forth.

# Feeling Blue

Brad is a friend of mine who was born blind. He does a lot of things that are remarkable. But he does one thing that is incredible. He can feel an object and tell me what color it is!

He isn't correct all of the time. Sometimes he says that a blue object is purple. Sometimes he's just totally wrong. But he is correct more often than not. I don't think his guesses are just luck. What do you think?

TEACHER'S KEY

Puzzle: "Feeling Blue"—Can humans actually feel colors?
Key Cognitive Skills: Designing experiments, speculating
Key Concepts: Nervous system, sensory apparatus
Difficulty Level: Relatively Easy
Sources of Information: See references 16 and 21.

Background Information and Solution

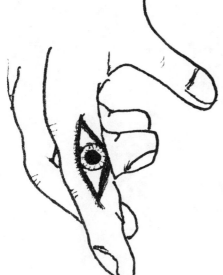

The point of this puzzler is to provide students with an introduction to designing their own experiments. The question here is whether humans have light sensors in parts of the body other than the eyes. Many lower animals have light sensors distributed throughout the body, so some evolutionary justification exists for asking this question. Scientific research on light sensors in the body has indicated that people may in fact be able to "see" colors with their fingertips.

Have students design some simple experiments to test this hypothesis. Have experimenters control as many variables as possible—making sure their subjects cannot see the test colors, using a variety of colors, wording their questions to the subjects as carefully as possible (no experimenter cues), and so forth. Discuss with the class how they will collect data and what measures they will use to interpret the data after the experiment. How will the experimenters know that the results are not due to "chance" or lucky guessing?

Libraries Unlimited, Inc. • P.O. Box 3988 • Englewood, CO 80155-3988

Nature Puzzlers (Lawrence E. Hillman)

SUGGESTED ADDITIONAL ACTIVITIES

1. The ability of music to evoke color (synesthesia) has been widely investigated. Try this experiment in your class. Play a short piece of music without lyrics. Ask students to close their eyes and write down the most dominant color elicited by the music. Then take a survey of the results. What is the color most often mentioned? Are the results fairly uniform among students or very diverse? Speculate about the connection between hearing and sight. Design some experiments that would help us understand synesthesia.

2. Do blind people have supernormal senses of hearing and touch? They probably do not. However, they are more motivated to react to sensory cues that most of us ignore. The same is true for many animals that rely on other senses to survive. Examine the vocabulary of human sensing by making a list (as a class) of words associated with the five senses. Which list has the most words and why? What aspects of hearing, touch, taste, and smell have no words associated with them? Can words be invented for these sensory modalities? How would such words come into common usage?

3. Have students read a story in which the main character has lost one or more senses. Discuss how this person copes with life.

4. Many animals live in environments that are entirely dark, such as in caves or at extreme ocean depths. Have students hypothesize about the structure and behavior of these animals. Would they need to have different colors? If they are blind, how do they get around? Then have students test these predictions by researching animals that do live in these environments. How close were the predictions to actual fact? See references 16 and 21.

Misguided Salmon

July 5, 1987

The Department of Fisheries reported today that many Atlantic salmon are not returning to their home streams to spawn. For thousands of years, newly hatched salmon have found their way from streambed to sea, developed to maturity in the ocean, and returned to their birthplace to spawn and die in a never-ending cycle. However, scientists at the University of Maine report that during recent years schools of salmon have failed to return to their home streams.

The reason for this sudden change of habit is still unknown. Scientists are unwilling to speculate about causes until more information can be obtained.

Libraries Unlimited, Inc. • P.O. Box 3988 • Englewood, CO 80155-3988   *Nature Puzzlers* (Lawrence E. Hillman)

TEACHER'S KEY

Puzzle: "Misguided Salmon"—Why aren't salmon finding their old spawning sites?
Key Cognitive Skills: Fact-finding, hypothesizing, deduction
Key Concepts: Migration, animal senses, environmental pollution
Difficulty Level: Relatively Easy
Sources of Information: See references 1, 4, 13, and 64.

Background Information and Solution

This puzzler is a good follow-up to other puzzlers involving animal senses. Students can research, guess, or be told how salmon find their way back to the stream where they were hatched—by sense of smell. Then students can hypothesize about causes that interrupt the sense of smell in the fish. Encourage students to explain the link between the cause and its effect on the salmon. For example, if students hypothesize that pollution is causing the fish to lose their sense of smell, then have the students research types of pollution that would be reasonable candidates and show a direct connection.

At the time of this writing, scientists think that acid rain is the major factor. Some scientists have experimented with the effect of acidic water on the sense of smell in fish and have found that the salmon's sense of smell was affected. Remind students that no one correct answer to this puzzle exists. The point of the puzzle is to have students make some reasonable hypotheses about causes and attempt to find some reasonable connections between cause and effect.

Alternate Hypotheses

1. Salmon follow the scent of the lead fish in the school. The lead fishes are being captured by fishermen and the result is that the remaining fish cannot find their way back to the spawning grounds. This hypothesis does not explain how the lead fish would find its way back.

2. Garbage dumped into the ocean from nearby cities masks the smell that the fish follow. This is a good hypothesis, but it assumes that spawning streams are near major cities or that the garbage is transported by ocean currents into the vicinity of stream outwashes. Have students research these assumptions.

SUGGESTED ADDITIONAL ACTIVITIES

1. Acid rain has been a much researched and controversial topic. Have students investigate the causes, effects, and suggested "cures" for the acid rain problem. Ask students to brainstorm some creative ways of solving the problem that would satisfy industry, recreation, and resource managers. In particular, discuss the meaning of the word "cost" (both financial and environmental). Also ask students to investigate how acid rain affects the relationships between countries.

2. How might one go about experimenting with the effects of acid rain on a lake? Have students design some experiments that would help answer this question. A good way to approach this problem is to generate more specific questions about the problem. How does acidity affect plants? Are all plants affected? What changes occur in the food chain? How are fish affected? How are the animals affected that eat the fish?

3. National parks have an incredible problem with pollution from park visitors—people trampling vegetation, cars giving off exhausts, trash that can mame or kill animals, people carving their initials on trees, and so forth. One park ranger—turned author—at one time suggested the following solution to this growing problem: Close the park roads to all traffic, including bicycles and horses. If people want to visit the parks, they can visit the parks on foot, entering from any trail or road that leads to the outside. This practice will return the parks to near wilderness status by diminishing the amount of terrain that can be covered in a day and thus "expanding" the park. Have students debate this solution.

4. Ask students to write a newspaper article on some form of pollution in their city or town. How unbiased should the article be? Should it attempt to persuade readers one way or the other? Or, should the article simply state objective facts?

Soldiers

In the biology classroom, my teacher keeps red ants in a huge terrarium. A couple of large beetles live in the tunnels with the ants, but the ants don't seem to mind much. They just crawl over the beetles and ignore them.

Then one day I watched the teacher feed the ants. He took a large beetle — the same kind that lives in the terrarium — and placed it carefully on the surface of the soil in the tank. Almost instantly, ants came to the surface from beneath the soil and killed the beetle. Then, they took the beetle into one of the tunnels and stored it for food.

A couple of days later, the new beetle had been eaten. But the beetles that were living with the ants were unharmed.

I just don't understand! Why don't the ants eat the beetles living in the terrarium?

Libraries Unlimited, Inc. • P.O. Box 3988 • Englewood, CO 80155-3988   *Nature Puzzlers* (Lawrence E. Hillman)

TEACHER'S KEY

Puzzle: "Soldiers" — Why don't ants eat beetles living in their terrarium?
Key Cognitive Skills: Comparing and contrasting, hypothesizing, deduction
Key Concepts: Chemical communication
Difficulty Level: Relatively Easy
Sources of Information: See references 7, 34, and 65.

Background Information and Solution

This problem is about differences and should be approached in that manner. Ask students to compare and contrast the beetles in the tunnels with the beetle placed in the tank by the teacher. Obviously, students need not focus on physical descriptions of the beetles since they are of the same species. Differences, other than physical, will form the basis for hypothesizing. For example, one difference was that the lone beetle was handled by the teacher. Thus, one hypothesis might state that the smell of the teacher's hand produced the attack. Additional hypotheses are listed below.

When students have presented a reasonable number of tentative hypotheses, ask them to provide ways of testing the hypotheses one-by-one. When the students have provided an acceptable test for one hypothesis, proceed by saying, "OK. That's good, but let's suppose now that this prediction didn't happen. How can we test the next hypothesis?" Continue until all the various hypotheses have been discussed. The point here is to involve students in thinking of forming hypotheses and then making predictions that can be checked in fact.

When all of the possible hypotheses have been exhausted, remind students that they may be assuming that ants react only by sight. Another sense may be involved. This suggestion will generate another series of hypotheses from which a series of suggested tests and predictions can be made.

When the sense of smell has been finally implicated, ask students again to suggest possible tests and predictions that would verify the following hypotheses: The ants recognize each other by the sense of smell. Since the beetles living with the ants in the tunnels have picked up the smell of the ants, the ants think the beetles are just one of them. Therefore, they don't attack those beetles.

Alternate Hypotheses

1. The ants do not attack the beetles in the tunnels because the ants are outnumbered by the bigger beetles.

2. The ants attack only animals on the surface, not ones underground.

3. The beetle placed in the tank showed fear. The ants can sense fear and attacked the beetle.

SUGGESTED ADDITIONAL ACTIVITIES

1. Place a number on the blackboard, for example "2," and tell students that you are going to put up more numbers according to some rule. Students have to discover the rule you are using (hypothesizing) and then predict the next number you will put on the board (testing the hypothesis).

The game will continue until students are able to state the rule and make correct predictions. Here are some good series of numbers to use for this exercise:

a. 1, 3, 7 ... (twice the previous number plus 1)

b. 0, 1, 1, 2, 3, 5, 8, 13 ... (add the two previous numbers to get the next number)

c. B, C, D, G ... (all the letters have a rounded part)

d. Billy, Joanne, George, Paul, Dina ... (names of students in alphabetical order according to last name)

2. Every adaptation has its advantages and disadvantages. For the ants in this puzzler, chemical means of species recognition has the one disadvantage of causing the ants to overlook a food supply that is literally right "under their noses." Have students list both the advantages and other disadvantages for the ants of this means of communication? Do the advantages outweigh the disadvantages? If not, how would one explain the fact that this form of communication is both common and ancient?

3. Even in humans, smell is a powerful means of communication. A strong connection exists between smell and memory, for instance. Certain smells can bring back long forgotten memories. Experiment with various smells (orange, perfume, etc.) in the classroom and have students report on the memories that the smells invoke. Have students hypothesize about the connection between smell and memory. What adaptive significance, if any, exists in this connection for humans now or in our evolutionary past? Have students begin to research this question by reading reference 34. Encourage students to research other connections of human smell.

It was my first day on the job. My assignment was to fly the helicopter route along the natural gas pipeline with Carl Rand, a government oil and gas engineer. We were looking for gas leaks along the pipeline. Leaks can be both dangerous and costly.

But spotting gas leaks isn't easy. First, natural gas is colorless, so we can't see the leaks. Second, the gas is also odorless—so we can't smell it. The engineers at the rig mix a smelly chemical with the gas before it goes into the pipeline, but we can't smell it from the helicopter. And we can't land the helicopter, because the forest is too thick in most places.

Time after time, Carl was able to spot leaks in the pipe. I tried to look for holes in the pipe, but even with binoculars I couldn't see any. I asked Carl to explain how he found the leaks. He just smiled and said, "You can figure it out. You're just not looking in the right place!"

Libraries Unlimited, Inc. • P.O. Box 3988 • Englewood, CO 80155-3988   *Nature Puzzlers* (Lawrence E. Hillman)

TEACHER'S KEY

Puzzle: "The Right Place"—How does an engineer spot gas leaks?
Key Cognitive Skills: Deduction
Key Concepts: Animal senses
Difficulty Level: Relatively Easy
Sources of Information: See reference 12.

Background Information and Solution

The key clue in this puzzle is the "smelly chemical" placed into the gas before it goes through the pipeline. The smell of this chemical, ethyl mercaptan, is familiar to anyone who has smelled gas coming from a gas stove or gas furnace. The chemical is placed there for safety reasons. The engineers looking for the leaks cannot smell the gas from the helicopter. So how does this chemical help them in their search? The logical deduction must be that something else is drawn to the smell. One hypothesis might be that a scavenger is drawn to the smell. What scavenger can be seen from a helicopter? It must be either a large individual scavenger that is drawn to every leak along the pipeline—unlikely—or a scavenger that "hunts" in large numbers, is relatively plentiful, and has easy access to various parts of the pipeline. The animal that fits these criteria is the vulture. A vulture has an incredibly acute sense of smell for incredibly bad smells. Carl looked up (rather than down) for the gas leaks.

Alternate Hypotheses

1. The gas killed animals in the vicinity of the leaks. This hypothesis violates common sense about natural gas. Small amounts in the open air are not deadly.

2. Flames are coming from the pipeline. This hypothesis assumes a way to ignite the gas at every point of leakage. This practice is unlikely, especially in the forest or tundra.

SUGGESTED ADDITIONAL ACTIVITIES

1. Encourage students to use the library media center to research the controversy over the Alaskan pipeline. Can human engineering and wilderness really coexist as some people imply? Are these two ideas mutually exclusive as others believe? Debate this issue in class. Do not ask students to "take sides." Instead, encourage students to collect facts and opinions on many sides of the issue and use this information to deduce the long term consequences of several different positions.

2. The puzzle gives one way of spotting gas leaks in a pipeline. However, wildlife biologists argue (quite reasonably) that using ethyl mercaptan to attract vultures to leaks is "unfair" to the vulture. The smell of the chemical makes the vulture use up valuable energy for a useless (to the vulture) task—energy that is needed for an already difficult type of existence. The question can therefore be submitted: "What other ways of detecting gas leaks can be used that would not affect wildlife?" Ask students to brainstorm some creative methods for detecting gas leaks that would not endanger plants or animals.

3. Here is an interesting research question that can teach students a great deal about ecology. The Water Board wants to build a small dam in the prairie about fifty miles east of the Rocky Mountain foothills in Colorado. The lake that results will be approximately nine miles in circumference. The water will be used to supply nearby towns during the dry season—July through September. Environmentalists, however, are complaining that the dam will damage the prairie community. The Water Board decides to do an "environmental impact" study to determine the effect of the new lake. Will the new lake be beneficial or destructive to the nearby environment?

Shape of Things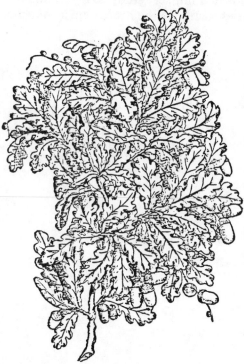

October 9, 1988

Mr. Larry Hillman
Academy School
Denver, CO 80222

Dear Mr. Hillman:

The other day, my five-year-old daughter brought some oak leaves into the house from our front yard. She was playing with the leaves on the kitchen table when she asked me why some of the leaves had a different shape from the others. We have only one oak tree in the front yard. It's the only oak tree on our block. So the leaves must have come from the same tree. I wish I could explain the difference to her, but the fact is, I just don't know! Since you teach biology to my older son, I thought maybe you could help me find the answer.

Sincerely,

Mary Lou Roberts

TEACHER'S KEY

Puzzle: "Shape of Things"—Why does a single oak tree have leaves of different shapes?
Key Cognitive Skills: Fact-finding, deduction, comparing by analogy
Key Concepts: Leaf physiology and structure
Difficulty Level: Relatively Easy
Sources of Information: See references 25 and 33.

Background Information and Solution

A large part of solving this problem is finding information on the "purposes" of a leaf—namely, photosynthesis and transpiration (releasing water). The students must then deduce how the shape of the leaf affects these functions—larger surface area means better ability to "catch" sunlight, and so forth. The final step in solving the puzzle is recognizing that leaves at the top of the oak tree live under slightly different conditions than the leaves down below. The leaves at the top receive more sunlight and wind than the leaves at the bottom. Therefore, the leaves at the bottom need to gather more light and transpire more rapidly.

An interesting classroom exercise is to have students cut out oak leaf shapes from paper or collect actual oak leaves if available and attempt to determine which leaf shapes have the most surface area. The greater the surface area, the more ability the leaf has to photosynthesize and transpire.

Alternate Hypotheses

1. Insects have eaten part of some leaves and thus changed the leaf's shape. This hypothesis is easily refuted by simple fact-finding. Many books that show oak leaves show the leaf variation for single species. Therefore, leaf variation is a normal occurrence and not the result of disease or insects.

2. The tree in this woman's front yard is actually two species of oak trees that have grown together to form one tree. Since different species of oak trees often have differences in growth requirements, this hypothesis is probably not true. Students can investigate the growth requirements (and habitats) of various species of oak trees to determine the likelihood of such an occurrence.

SUGGESTED ADDITIONAL ACTIVITIES

1. Have students compare and contrast the top and bottom leaves of a number of different plants and trees. Encourage students to attempt to explain any differences that occur. When no visible differences occur, ask students also to try to explain this observation.

2. In biology, many structures are explained at least partially by their function. For example, the shape of a deer's ear is explained at least partially by its function in detecting the approach of predators. Differences in function between species can, therefore, be associated with differences in structure. Have students compare the eye of an animal of their choice with a human eye and explain the differences and similarities between the two in terms of function. References in the library media center should provide the necessary information.

3. Ask students to research the environment of Mars. Then have them write an essay on "How to Build a Martian," basing the looks of the Martian on the premise that its structure reflects its environment.

4. How would one attempt to answer these questions: "What makes the oak leaves change form at the top and bottom of the tree?" "Do the differences in the environments at the top and bottom of the tree cause the leaves to grow differently?" "Does heredity determine the structure of the leaf?" "Is the difference in structure due to some combination of heredity and environment?" Discuss with students the processes needed to find the answers to these questions—experimentation, observations, and so forth.

Libraries Unlimited, Inc. • P.O. Box 3988 • Englewood, CO 80155-3988 *Nature Puzzlers* (Lawrence E. Hillman)

The Bird with ESP

The bird in this picture does something quite unusual. In years when not much food is available (it eats caterpillars), the bird produces two or three eggs. In years with plenty of food, it produces three to four eggs. Now that's not so unusual. What is unusual is that the bird seems to know beforehand if the caterpillars will be plentiful and when they are going to hatch. The time of year that the caterpillars hatch can change from year to year by as much as a month or more. But, the young birds always seem to hatch at the same time as the caterpillars.

How can the bird know when the caterpillars will hatch?

TEACHER'S KEY

Puzzle: "The Bird with ESP"—How does a bird know about some things before they happen?
Key Cognitive Skills: Hypothesizing
Key Concepts: Environmental cues
Difficulty Level: Relatively Easy
Sources of Information: See references 40, 45, and 57.

Background Information and Solution

The fact that scientists are not sure of the answer to this puzzler ensures that students cannot "look up the answer." What is important in this puzzler is creating hypotheses. The class should begin with the assumption that ESP is not at work here and focus on environmental cues that would possibly trigger physiological mechanisms and behavior (such as stimulating hormones and mating behavior). Emphasize the process of forming testable hypotheses.

Libraries Unlimited, Inc. • P.O. Box 3988 • Englewood, CO 80155-3988   *Nature Puzzlers* (Lawrence E. Hillman)

Alternate Hypotheses

1. The bird can count the number of caterpillar eggs on branches of trees. This hypothesis is probably not testable.

2. Spring temperatures affect both caterpillar egg production and the mating of the birds so the two events occur simultaneously. This hypothesis is excellent. Have students mention some ways that it could be tested.

SUGGESTED ADDITIONAL ACTIVITIES

1. Environmental cues (light, temperature, humidity, etc.) play an important role in the animal and plant worlds. Have students research information on photoperiodism in both plants and animals in general and then report individually on a particular animal or plant of their choice that exhibits this phenomenon. See reference 57.

2. Some humans are allegedly affected by the short days of winter—not by the cold but by the decrease in the number of hours of daylight. These people become irritable, restless, and sometimes unproductive. Suppose we hypothesize that this response happens to everyone in some degree or another. How could this hypothesis be tested? See reference 45.

3. Have students create some hypotheses concerning the hibernation of black bears. What causes hibernation—temperature, light, or the build up of carbon dioxide in the bears' dens? Have students create some hypotheses and explain how these hypotheses might be tested.

4. Are people really affected by rainy days? Is the reaction all in the person's mind or do other reasons exist? Follow this procedure as an on-going exercise. Have students keep a record, in a diary format, of their afternoon moods from day to day for a week. Keep your own record on the daily afternoon weather. At the end of the week, take a survey of the students' moods and write them on the chalkboard in categories determined by the students. Determine if any correlation exists between the afternoon moods of students and the next day's weather.

Nature Puzzlers II
Moderately Difficult

Predictions

The storm was so violent I didn't think we were going to live! My little sister huddled in the corner of the tent crying on my mother's shoulder. Even Dad—an experienced woodsman—looked scared. We were in a wilderness pine forest ten miles from our car. We couldn't just run home!

I peeked out of the tent window and saw lightning bolts striking the mountain ridges to the west. The thunder was so loud it hurt our ears. Then the wind began to blow. Rain came pouring down! We shut the tent windows and climbed into our warm sleeping bags as the lightning began to flash around us. I thought I heard lightning strike a tree near our tent. I could hear trees crashing to the ground during the night. I hoped that the trees over our tent were strong enough to stand the force of the wind.

The next morning we climbed out of the tent feeling wet and tired. As we looked around the campsite, we could see many fallen pine trees. Even many healthy trees were uprooted from the ground. Nearly one out of every ten trees had been blown over during the night.

My father looked very sad. He said that even though the storm had done little damage now, the whole forest was probably going to die within the next few years. I didn't believe him!

Three years later my dad and I came back to the same area for a day hike. I couldn't believe what I saw! Although the trees were standing, most of them were dead. Even the living trees were oozing sap and losing needles— soon to die with the rest of them. My father had been right! But how could he possibly have known?

TEACHER'S KEY

Puzzle: "Predictions"—How can a person predict the destruction of a forest by beetles long before it happens?

Key Cognitive Skills: Hypothesizing, predicting through deduction

Key Concepts: Environmental change

Difficulty Level: Moderately Difficult

Sources of Information: See reference 19.

Libraries Unlimited, Inc. • P.O. Box 3988 • Englewood, CO 80155-3988   *Nature Puzzlers* (Lawrence E. Hillman)

Background Information and Solution

The fallen trees created a safe breeding place for pine beetles—beetles that destroy pine trees. Ordinarily, woodpeckers feed on these beetles, and keep the beetle populations in check. However, the woodpeckers are unable to reach the beetles concealed by fallen trees. An unchecked beetle population can destroy a forest in several years' time. Oozing sap is one clue to the presence of pine beetles.

Approach this problem with students by asking for hypotheses and predictions based on the hypotheses. For example, the first hypothesis below predicts that the other trees would have been noticeably diseased before the storm. No clue in the puzzle says that this is the case. The second hypothesis below predicts that any forest would have soil erosion, since every forest has some fallen trees. Continue this process with other hypotheses suggested by students.

Alternate Hypotheses

1. The trees felled by the wind were diseased and spread the disease by contacting other trees when they fell.

2. The fallen trees exposed soil to the processes of erosion. During subsequent years, the soil eroded further and became depleted of nutrients—killing the remaining trees.

3. The trees that remained standing after the storm were exposed to excessive sun damage.

SUGGESTED ADDITIONAL ACTIVITIES

1. If the father knew that the forest was going to die, why didn't he try to do anything about it? Should he have told the Forest Service so they could spray insecticide to kill the beetles? Would human intervention have made matters worse? Discuss this option with the class.

    At the time of this writing, the National Park Service has a policy of noninterference with natural disasters within park boundaries. They would not have interfered with the beetle population in this instance. On the other hand, the National Forest Service does not have such a policy and may have interfered if they felt the situation warranted it. Discuss these two seemingly opposing positions with your class.

2. What other animals might have been affected by such a storm? What ecological effects might have followed? For example, how might the woodpecker population have been affected by the fallen trees? What other birds might have been affected? What other animals might have used the fallen trees for shelter? How would the additional sunlight emitted through the trees change life on the forest floor? Have students research the answers to these questions and then write different possible scenarios for these conditions.

3. What kinds of succession would you expect to find in this dead forest of pines? How will the wildlife change? What will happen to the soil, water runoff, and so forth?

4. Describe a specific climax community—one in which species diversity and numbers are fairly constant over large periods of time. Do climax communities really exist? What do we really mean by the "balance of nature" if the natural world is in a state of constant change?

5. Are some changes in nature better than others? If so, how do we know they are better? Should we make an effort to preserve wilderness? Why should we worry about such things as the ozone layer? Have students debate these issues in class. Invite people with varying views on these issues to talk to your class.

6. Most of the time the outcome of ecological changes—natural or otherwise—is difficult, if not impossible, to predict. To what extent can ecology aspire to be a "hard" science in the sense that physics is a hard science? How is ecology both a science and an art? What makes measurement and prediction so difficult in environmental science?

Libraries Unlimited, Inc. • P.O. Box 3988 • Englewood, CO 80155-3988   *Nature Puzzlers* (Lawrence E. Hillman)

Split Decisions

The plant you see in this picture is odd. The top half of the plant has flat, broad, green leaves on short stems. The bottom half of the plant has long, narrow, green leaves on long stems. The stalk of the upper half is thin and rigid. The stalk on the lower half is thicker, but less rigid.

In what type of environment does this plant live?

TEACHER'S KEY

Puzzle: "Split Decisions" — Why are the plant's leaves so unusual?
Key Cognitive Skills: Deduction, fact-finding, comparing and contrasting
Key Concepts: Leaf physiology and structure, environmental physiology
Difficulty Level: Moderately Difficult
Sources of Information: See references 25, 33, and sources on general botany or environmental plant physiology.

Background Information and Solution

This plant has two different leaf structures because it lives in two entirely different environments at the same time. It is a freshwater plant inhabiting streams and ponds. The upper half of the plant grows above the water surface; the lower half grows below the water surface. The result of this double existence is two very different types of body plan. Each structure meets the requirements of a different environment.

Solving this problem requires students to think through the relationship between leaf structure and the problems a plant faces as part of its survival. Looking at a large variety of plants in different environments will help students begin to see this relationship. For example, they will discover that the lower leaves are typical of water plants. They have a large surface area which is needed to secure oxygen from the water and light from the sun.

Alternate Hypotheses

1. The plant was found in a meadow with dense vegetation. The lower leaves were shaded by the sun.

2. This plant is a parasitic plant. The bottom part is used to attach the plant firmly to the branches of a tree.

3. The plant was found on a sand dune. The bottom leaves are dwarfed because they are sometimes covered with shifting sands.

SUGGESTED ADDITIONAL ACTIVITIES

1. Why would the lower leaves be narrower than the upper leaves? Why is increased surface area of the underwater leaves necessary? What problems does a plant face living partly underwater? Have students use the library media center to answer these and other questions about aquatic plants.

2. The leaves above the water surface have stomata, guard cells, and an abundance of woody tissue. The underwater leaves have none of these structures. Furthermore, the underwater leaves show little or no differentiation in cell type in contrast to the aerial cells. How would you explain these differences? Attempt to explain these variations through class discussion.

3. How might a scientist determine whether the leaf variation on this plant is genetic or environmentally induced? Have students suggest some experiments that might provide some clues to this problem.

4. Obtain some aquarium plants and some common lawn plants (weeds, grass, and so forth). Have students compare and contrast both the general form and detailed anatomy of these plants. What general principles can be drawn regarding leaf structure in aerial and aquatic environments?

5. The aquatic environment poses an entirely different set of problems for living things than the aerial environment. Have students do research on the anatomical differences between land and sea animals. For example, encourage students to compare and contrast the anatomy of a whale and a human. Ask students to make connections between environment and anatomical structure.

 Patterns

Sometimes you come across something that's totally weird. And this one has me baffled!

As my family hiked along an old mining road near Peaceful Valley, my sister stopped suddenly and called to us. She pointed to something lying near the bank of a stream that followed the road.

"They're just some old pine needles," my mother said.

"I know that," my sister said. "But look how they are arranged. Pine needles just don't fall from a tree into patterns like this."

We had to admit that she was right about that. The needles were piled about a half-inch high, four inches wide, and formed criss-crossing patterns similar to the picture on this page. The lines of criss-crossing pine needles continued off the road and into the forest for about 200 feet.

"I think an animal did it," my sister said. She lifted a section of pine needles and looked at them carefully. The section was not hollow so it couldn't have been a tunnel. The ground below the needles was not disturbed.

"No," my father said. "Why would an animal lay down a bunch of pine needles? I think they were washed down the road when the stream overflowed last spring."

That brought a comment from my mother, "If that were true, wouldn't we see some gullies made by the rushing water? I don't see any gullies, do you?"

Well, once again my sister has started an argument! But at least this time it's about something interesting—at least interesting enough to keep us arguing about it at the dinner table. I would really like to know the answer, but I'm not sure I ever will.

TEACHER'S KEY

Puzzle: "Patterns"—What caused strange pine needle patterns on a forest road?
Key Cognitive Skills: Deduction
Key Concepts: Behavioral adaptation to environment
Difficulty Level: Moderately Difficult
Sources of Information: See references 21 and 36.

Libraries Unlimited, Inc. • P.O. Box 3988 • Englewood, CO 80155-3988   *Nature Puzzlers* (Lawrence E. Hillman)

Background Information and Solution

These patterns were created by small rodents, voles, that burrow through the snow during the winter. The voles often line their snow tunnels with vegetation, presumably for warmth or food. When the snow melts, the remaining stored vegetation retains the shape of the original tunnels—which criss-crossed beneath the winter snow.

Alternate Hypotheses

1. Wind blew the needles into this pattern. The needles collected in eddies created by the trees and stream bank.

2. Runoff from rains washed the needles into this pattern.

3. These patterns were originally small animal trails. The pine needles were packed down as a result of animals walking on them. Loose needles nearby were blown away by wind or washed away by water leaving the patterns that we see now.

SUGGESTED ADDITIONAL ACTIVITIES

1. The sister hypothesized, "I think an animal did it." What makes this statement a very poor hypothesis? How could it be reworded to make a better hypothesis? Is the father's hypothesis more clearly stated? How could it be improved?

2. An hypothesis may be denied as a result of evidence to the contrary. Does the mother present enough evidence to falsify the father's hypothesis (that stream overflow created the pine needle patterns)? What other types of evidence would one look for in order to verify or falsify this hypothesis?

3. Design an experiment that might test the father's hypothesis.

4. Animals leave many signs of their presence in the woods besides tracks. Suppose we accept the given solution of this puzzle as a probable, but nonetheless, conditional hypothesis. Remembering that scientists must look for evidence that might falsify an hypothesis, what indirect evidence (or lack of evidence) might we look for in the forest to refute the solution? What additional evidence would increase the probability of its being true?

5. Encourage students to use the library media center to research other burrowing animals that live in pine forests. How do these animals use vegetation in their tunnels or burrows?

Libraries Unlimited, Inc. • P.O. Box 3988 • Englewood, CO 80155-3988   *Nature Puzzlers* (Lawrence E. Hillman)

Balancing Act

Our "backyard" is a whole national forest. We have lots of wild birds eating out of the feeder near our house.

One night, my father and a neighbor were bragging to each other about things each of them could do better than the other. Finally, Mr. Baldwin said, "I know I can do something that you can't do!"

"Oh, yeah. What's that?" my father asked.

"You won't believe this, but I can make one of those wild birds in your backyard stand on one leg for a minute without ever having to train him to do it."

"Sure," my father said. "And can you make him whistle the 'Star Spangled Banner' at the same time?"

"I knew you wouldn't believe me," said Mr. Baldwin.

"I not only don't believe you, but I'll cut the grass in your front lawn for a month if you can make a wild bird do that! But if you can't do it, you have to cut the grass in my front lawn for a month. Is it a deal?"

This past Saturday I was leaving the house to go to softball practice. I saw Mr. Baldwin heading toward our house with a small tape recorder and a stereo speaker. That afternoon when I came home, my father was cutting Mr. Baldwin's front lawn.

TEACHER'S KEY

Puzzle: "Balancing Act"—How can a man make a wild bird stand on one leg using a tape recorder and speaker?

Key Cognitive Skills: Hypothesizing, questioning

Key Concepts: Territory, releasing stimuli

Difficulty Level: Moderately Difficult

Sources of Information: See references 40 and 67.

Background Information and Solution

Most students will figure out quickly that the tape recorder and speaker are used to play a bird song. However, they will have more difficulty realizing that the bird song that is playing is the bird's

Libraries Unlimited, Inc. • P.O. Box 3988 • Englewood, CO 80155-3988   *Nature Puzzlers* (Lawrence E. Hillman)

own song—taped beforehand using the same tape recorder. The most difficult part of solving the puzzle, though, is figuring out how a bird's own song can make it stand on one leg.

In order to solve this last part of the puzzle, students must discover that bird songs are used to establish territories by warning other birds of the same species to stay away. When Frank Baldwin played back the bird's own song, the bird interpreted it as an intruder in its territory. The bird, having located the source of the sound, attempted to attack the speaker to drive it from the territory. But Frank knew something about bird behavior in this situation. He knew that the bird would attack or retreat depending on the volume of the song coming from the speaker (just as it would with a real bird of its own species). By raising and lowering the volume on the speaker, Frank made the bird attack or retreat at will. The bird was so attuned to reacting to these volume levels that when Frank discovered the critical volume, he suspended the bird between attacking and retreating and left the bird literally standing on one leg. The biologist William Dilger, first attempted this feat with wood thrushes and was quite successful.

One way to approach this problem in the classroom is to use a "questions" approach. Students can frame questions to ask the teacher, but the teacher can respond only with a "yes" or "no" answer. When students don't ask a question in the yes or no format, the teacher may respond with "You're on the right track." or "You're getting colder." but not answer the question directly.

Alternate Hypotheses

Students will attempt a number of wild and improbable hypotheses. Some students will have Mr. Baldwin stunning the bird with loud sounds or hypnotizing it with soft music. As crazy as some hypotheses might be, seriously consider them without negative judgment. This exercise is good for developing creative thinking.

SUGGESTED ADDITIONAL ACTIVITIES

1. Dog trainers know that dogs can be trained more easily to do things that closely resemble their natural behaviors. For example, teaching a wolf to "shake hands" is much easier than teaching a wolf to "sit." Wolves use pawing motions as part of their natural communication with other wolves; whereas, sitting is not a natural activity for wolves. This principle can be applied to training a host of other animals as well. As a class, apply the above principle to this question: "How would you train an elephant to carry logs?"

2. In the puzzler, a bird call of the same species was adequate to make another bird attack or retreat. In biology, a stimulus that brings about an automatic response in an animal is known as a "releaser." What kinds of "releasers" work for humans?

3. Some people claim that a large part of human behavior is hereditary. Have students research and write about similarities they see between their own behavior and that of their parents. Then discuss ways of finding out whether this behavior is inherited or learned. Since, the answer to these questions are still "up in the air" even for scientists, this exercise provides the use of many problem-solving skills.

A Cute Angle

You've probably heard the saying, "Beauty is in the eyes of the beholder." But when it comes to cute, babies seem to have it over all of us. This advantage is just as true for animals as it is for humans.

Many mammals respond to certain features in their babies that trigger the "parental instinct." Most people would agree that some of the animals shown are "cuter" than others. What facial features do the "cute" animals share that the older adults don't seem to have?

Make a collection of animal pictures and see if you can tell what makes an animal cute.

Libraries Unlimited, Inc. • P.O. Box 3988 • Englewood, CO 80155-3988   *Nature Puzzlers* (Lawrence E. Hillman)

TEACHER'S KEY

Puzzle: "A Cute Angle" — What does it mean to be "cute"?
Key Cognitive Skills: Comparing and contrasting, defining by operationalizing, measurement
Key Concepts: Stimulus response, behavioral releasers
Difficulty Level: Moderately Difficult
Sources of Information: See reference 62.

Background Information and Solution

Students will vary somewhat as to their criteria of cuteness. A class vote on the cuteness of the animals in the puzzle will usually show that certain stimuli evoke the "awwww ..." reaction. Have students go through magazines, books, comic strips, and so forth and assemble a collection of pictures that vary from "cute" to "ugly." Start with qualitative definitions such as "button nose" and move gradually to more operational definitions such as "distance from corner of eye to tip of nose." Once a set of qualitative and quantitative criteria have been established, move to the additional activities to test these criteria.

In general, students will discover the following "releasers" or "stimuli" for the "parental instinct": short faces, round eyes, prominent forehead, round cheeks, and less prominent chin. Students should then try to operationalize these criteria by actually measuring distances between features on the face and collecting data on animals that range from "cute" to "ugly." Specify exactly how the measurements are to be made. Ask students to justify their decisions.

Alternate Hypotheses

The hypotheses that students present should be precisely stated criteria for cuteness. The following are just two examples of possible hypotheses: "As the nose becomes longer, the animal seems to be less cute." and "In a cute animal, the eyes are bigger in proportion to the head."

SUGGESTED ADDITIONAL ACTIVITIES

1. Students tend to assume that measurement implies using only a ruler. As students discuss their measurement techniques, address this assumption and suggest that other ways to measure might exist. In addition, brainstorm ways of making difficult measurements such as the "roundness of eyes" (ellipses) or the "shape" of the nose. These are excellent exercises in creativity and ingenuity.

2. Have students choose a number of pictures that vary in cuteness on a scale of one to ten based on some criteria of measurement. For example, number one might be "just plain ugly" and have none of the criteria. Number 2 might be "only a mother could love" and have only one of the measured criteria — for example, a prominent forehead — but none of the other features. Number 3 might have two of the criteria and so forth up to number 10 — "really, really cute." Then have each student show the pictures to one male and female family member, asking each to rate each picture on a scale of one to ten. Compare the class results.

3. Ask students to choose one of the following concepts and write a short article on making the concept as exact as possible (operationalize the concept). Explain that no specific people are to be mentioned in the article—only how you would make the determination. Criteria should be both qualitative and quantitative.

a. the best football player in the National Football League

b. the nicest person in the school

c. the best friend a person could possibly have

d. the stupidest dog in the universe

Unfriendly Neighbors

I've heard of people who don't get along. I've heard of animals that don't get along. But I had never heard of plants that don't like each other until...

Well, let me start at the beginning. My family and I went camping in July in Rocky Mountain National Park. One day my father had the bright idea of going on one of those nature walks—you know, the kind where a ranger tells you about plants and animals and everything. We hiked in this area that didn't have any trees and was real high up—over 11,000 feet.

Anyway, the ranger showed us two plants that just refused to live together. One plant was called "phlox" and the other was called "primrose." Whenever you saw one kind of plant growing in an area you couldn't find the other kind of plant mixed in with it. The two plants, however, had other types of plants living with them. Only the phlox and primrose seemed not to like each other. At least that's the way it seemed.

The ranger explained why the two plants don't live together. But I don't think anybody was listening because we were all getting a bad sunburn and the wind was cold.

We made it back to our cars, stepping around the other tiny plants in the area and the few patches of snow left on the ground from winter. That short trip wasn't easy—we were all out of breath when we got back to the cars. Even my brother, the "basketball star," was tired.

I wish now that I had listened when the ranger was talking, because it bugs me not knowing the answer. I do remember that the answer seemed short, so it couldn't be too hard to figure out.

TEACHER'S KEY

Puzzle: "Unfriendly Neighbors"— Why do two plants "refuse" to live together?
Key Cognitive Skills: Deduction, fact-finding
Key Concepts: Micro-environments, plant growth requirements, tundra life zone
Difficulty Level: Moderately Difficult
Sources of Information: See references 23, 41, 43, 47, and 68.

Background Information and Solution

The alpine tundra of the Rocky Mountains is a high-altitude (usually above 10,000 feet), wind-swept, cold, and treeless environment consisting mostly of dwarf vegetation. The growing season is very short; snow covers the soil and temperatures fall below freezing from September through June.

In order to solve this problem, students must be able to make connections between the growth requirements of plants and variations within the tundra environment. Since the facts in the puzzle imply that wind, sunlight, and soil conditions are constant between the two species, some other factor such as moisture, plant competition, and so forth must be involved. The key to solving this puzzle is recognizing that the wind distributes snow in a patchwork pattern. As a result, temperature and moisture conditions in the spring vary considerably within just a few feet. Phlox tends to inhabit the more exposed areas where wind has blown the ground free of snow. Primula, or primrose, is found in areas where snow cover has remained longer into the spring. This conjecture then can be further researched by predicting other mutually exclusive species on the tundra.

Alternate Hypotheses

1. Each plant produces a "poison" in the soil that prevents the other plant from growing next to it. This situation actually does occur with some species of plants, but in this case, the plants at the edge of each circle of growth are growing next to each other.

2. The seeds of the two plants are distributed by different means. The phlox drops its seeds in the area where it's growing. The primula distributes its seeds by wind. Again this is an interesting hypothesis. However, since the wind on the tundra is nearly constant and usually strong, wind-carried seeds probably will be evenly distributed over the ground. Thus, the primrose seeds would invade the phlox's territory.

SUGGESTED ADDITIONAL ACTIVITIES

1. Research other situations in which plants are exclusive due to environmental factors. Some examples might be differences in tree species on the north and south sides of a mountain, differences in tree species at 9,000 feet and 6,000 feet in altitude, and differences between plants that live on a sand dune near the ocean and those that live on a sand dune in the desert.

2. Plants are known to "communicate" with each other. Have students research ways that plants communicate with each other or with animals. Some plants, for instance, actually emit high frequency sounds when under drought conditions; some insects are able to pick up these frequencies. Speculate on how this relationship might be beneficial to both the insects and the plant. Encourage students to write humorous stories about what plants might "say" to each other.

3. One interesting feature of alpine tundra plants is that their colors are often intense. Flowers generally are brightly colored or deeply shaded. The leaves and stems are generally very dark green. Ask students to explain these facts, relating the colors to some environmental factor. (The bright colors and dark green absorb more heat, thus increasing the plant's metabolism in a cold environment.) Have students infer (deduce) some other adaptations of plants that live in a

windy, cold environment—examples include fuzzy stems, basal leaves with a lot of area exposed to the sun, and so forth. Research these predictions by reporting on the characteristics of known tundra plants.

4. Have students try to predict differences and similarities in structure between tundra plants on north, south, east, and west slopes of a mountain. For example, if the west side of the mountain is generally windier than the east side of the mountain, how might this affect the sizes of plants, their color, and so forth?

I go fishing often. I've fished in Lake Ontario and the Atlantic Ocean. I've fished in reservoirs in New Jersey and I've fished in the Mississippi River. In every one of those places I've seen a dead fish at some time or another.

Last month I went on vacation to Colorado and I fished in ten different lakes, including two reservoirs, in Summit County. During that whole month I didn't see one dead fish in a lake or stream (except, of course, the ones that I caught). I asked one of the local people if he knew why there weren't any dead fish in the lakes. The wise-guy said, "Cause they live forever." There has got to be a better answer than that.

Libraries Unlimited, Inc. • P.O. Box 3988 • Englewood, CO 80155-3988   *Nature Puzzlers* (Lawrence E. Hillman)

TEACHER'S KEY

Puzzle: "Fishing for Answers"—Where have all the dead fish gone (at least in the mountains)?
Key Cognitive Skills: Deduction, comparing and contrasting
Key Concepts: Process of decay and recycling in nature, byproducts of decay
Difficulty Level: Moderately Difficult
Sources of Information: See reference 31.

Background Information and Solution

Solving this puzzle involves students in making some remote connections. The teacher may want to guide students through this puzzle a little more gently than others for two reasons: because the deductions and relationships are not as direct as in other puzzles, and because talk about "decay" and "death" is unpleasant for some students.

Remind students that death and decay are necessary processes in the natural world and that if decay did not take place, the world would be more unpleasant than a smelly fish. With this taken care of, the teacher may gently guide students (by judicious questioning) through the following chain of reasoning.

"Let's assume that the fish are not washed downstream since this information contradicts the fact that no dead fish were found in the mountain reservoirs. Some dead fish must exist in the mountain lakes. However, the fish in the mountain lakes are not floating to the water surface like the fish in the other lakes and rivers mentioned.

Now, what would cause a dead fish to float? Right, some sort of gas such as oxygen or carbon dioxide. How is this gas being made? Right again, through the process of bacterial decay. What factors can slow down or stop bacterial decay—temperature, sunlight, chemicals, and so forth?

OK, so now let's compare the 'dead fish' lakes with the 'no dead fish' lakes and see what the major differences are. Great. The answer is temperature. The mountain lakes are too cold for bacteria to work fast enough or work at all. So the fish just sink to the bottom and are devoured by scavengers. You all get A's today."

Alternate Hypotheses

1. Saltwater fish float to the surface because they have an air bladder and freshwater fish do not. This hypothesis is partially true but is easily refuted by the fact that the person in the story saw floating fish in New Jersey reservoirs and the Mississippi River—both bodies of fresh water.

2. Air pressure is less in the mountains and so dead fish in mountain lakes do not accumulate enough gas to float. This hypothesis is a good try, but the fact that air pressure is less in the mountains might have the exact opposite effect—it would take less gas to make the fish float.

Libraries Unlimited, Inc. • P.O. Box 3988 • Englewood, CO 80155-3988   *Nature Puzzlers* (Lawrence E. Hillman)

SUGGESTED ADDITIONAL ACTIVITIES

1. What would happen if everything and everybody lived forever? This question makes a great subject for a short story or essay.

2. How many times have you seen a dead bird? Have you ever wondered what happens to them? Does the same thing happen to other dead animals? How does this relate to the importance of scavengers?

3. Have students research various "recyclers" in nature—fungi, scavengers, molds, various insects, and so forth.

4. Decay is a source of frustration for those of us who try to preserve food. Research and discuss canning, curing, refrigeration, and so forth, and how they work to prevent decay.

5. Have students read reference 31. Experiment with miniature ecosystems in the class. Have students observe the ecosystems over a period of time and write about the processes of birth, death, and decay.

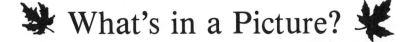 What's in a Picture?

Look at the picture of the bird. From looking at the picture, try to answer the following questions.

1. What does the bird eat?
2. Where does the bird eat? on the ground? in the air? in trees? in shallow water?
3. What method does the bird use to obtain its food?
4. Where does the bird build its nest?
5. What kind of climate does the bird live in?
6. Does the bird live in a forest or a meadow?
7. In what month of the year do the bird's eggs hatch?

Libraries Unlimited, Inc. • P.O. Box 3988 • Englewood, CO 80155-3988   *Nature Puzzlers* (Lawrence E. Hillman)

TEACHER'S KEY

Puzzle: "What's in a Picture"—How much can you learn about a bird from its picture?
Key Cognitive Skills: Deduction
Key Concepts: Structural adaptations
Difficulty Level: Moderately Difficult
Sources of Information: See reference 40.

Background Information and Solution

The bird in the picture is the red headed woodpecker. The point of this puzzler is to make deductions from observations. Have students observe carefully the various parts of the bird—its coloration, the shape of its beak, the shape and structure of its feet, the length of its wings, the placement of its eyes on the head, the texture of its feathers, and so forth. Tell students that these are clues to the bird's life. Students do not need to answer all the questions exactly. The focus of this puzzle is the process of deduction—how students came up with their answers. If the deduction is "reasonable," accept the answer—at least temporarily. Answers may change as new deductions are made.

For example, the wings are short enough to suggest that the bird lives in the forest—it needs short wings to fly through the tight spaces between trees. A student may suggest, however, that short wings could also be beneficial to meadow birds that nest in brush. Accept both deductions temporarily. Another student might point out that the beak is "spearlike" suggesting the bird might spear its food. Ask what kind of food needs to be "speared"? Students might answer insects under the ground. Ask if the bird's feet are designed for ground feeding? Continue in this manner until all of the bird's characteristics have been discussed.

The red headed woodpecker feeds on the side of trees by working its beak into the bark and capturing insects. It nests in holes made on the sides of trees and lays its eggs in the spring—the time of greatest food abundance.

SUGGESTED ADDITIONAL ACTIVITIES

1. Collect a number of pictures of various animals from various habitats. Using only the pictures, have students try to deduce the animal's habitat and habits.

2. Take a field trip to the local museum. If the museum has dinosaur bones, do an exercise similar to 1 above. Have students pay attention to features such as teeth, feet, and thickness of bones. Have students research the dinosaur's habitats and habits to verify their answers.

3. After having done exercises 1 and 2 above, have students make some generalizations about the most useful features of an animal for telling about its lifestyle.

4. This writing assignment aids in the understanding of deduction from observation, both in science and in art. As homework, have students write a detailed description of their own bedrooms. Explain to them that the objects they describe should be chosen so as to enable someone else reading the description to deduce whose room it is. This technique is used by novelists to subtly describe characters and moods through details of setting. The following day, read the descriptions to the class (without, of course, indicating the name of the student) and have students deduce the author or at least some traits about the author.

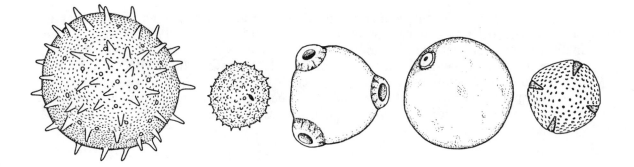

August 15, 1989

Small Business Association
1400 Cedar Street
Ft. Morgan, CO 80019

Dear Sirs:

We would like to apply for a business loan through your organization. Several associates and I would like to supply doctors in Colorado with pollen samples for use in allergy testing.

We believe that we have developed a method of pollen collection that is economical. The method consists of finding pure strands of ragweed, pine, and other plants with known allergens. Using portable vacuums and generators, the pollen is collected in large, sterile bags from each stand. The pollen can then be removed from these bags and shipped in sterile test tubes to allergists in the state.

Please forward to us an application for a business loan and any related materials. We appreciate your consideration and hope to hear from you soon.

Sincerely,

John Trudeau
Marc Hannon
Cecelia Martin

August 20, 1989

John Trudeau, Marc Hannon, and Cecelia Martin
11900 Common Way
Denver, CO 80122

Dear Sirs and Madam:

Although we are sending you an application for a loan, we must advise you that a local company offering a similar service to doctors went bankrupt in 1980. Since we were unable to collect on that loan, it is unlikely that your loan will be approved. Our advisers indicate that the demand for such a service is high. However, the method (similar to yours) of pollen collection used by the former company was inadequate. We suggest that you develop a better method of collecting pollen before considering a loan application.

Thank you for your interest in the Small Business Association. We wish you luck in your new venture.

Sincerely,

Thomas Main
Loan Officer

TEACHER'S KEY

Puzzle: "Small Business"—Can students develop a better method of collecting pollen than a would-be entrepreneur?
Key Cognitive Skills: Fact-finding, extrapolating
Key Concepts: Flower structure, types of pollen
Difficulty Level: Moderately Difficult
Sources of Information: See references 25, 33, and 57.

Background Information and Solution

Students can learn a great deal about the structure of flowers from this exercise. First, they should research the various types of pollen dispersal—wind, water, and insect—in order to grasp some of the overall differences in pollen structure, flower structure, and their relation to pollen dispersal. Obtain some old flowers from a florist or collect some flowers from neighborhood lots. Have students carefully dissect the flowers to identity major structures—particularly the anthers and other adaptations for pollination.

Once some overall information about flower structure and pollination has been collected, have students find information on several different allergenic plants and the pollens they produce. Have them select which varieties they wish to collect. Encourage them to find a method for collecting large quantities of the pollen. Emphasize the difficulties inherent in the "vacuum method" before brainstorming new methods. This discussion helps students to avoid duplicating these same problems. The vacuum method collects not only the desired pollen but also wind-blown pollen in the vicinity. In addition, a "pure" stand of any flower is difficult to find.

Alternate Hypotheses

The students' most common attempt at a solution is to macerate the entire flower and then separate the pollen from the mass. Unfortunately, this procedure is not practical as a business solution because it is very time consuming and too expensive.

SUGGESTED ADDITIONAL ACTIVITIES

1. Have students research how to write a business proposal. When research is complete have them write a proposal for starting a company that uses better methods of pollen collection. Some teachers have used a small group of students as a "review board" for evaluating proposals of other student groups applying for a "loan." Students communicate, via letter, about their proposals and ways to improve their methods. Students can then discuss, as a class, their proposed solutions, problems the solutions entail, and so forth.

2. Present the following problem to the class. Suppose you experienced an allergic reaction several times after eating dinner—say for seven successive days. How would you determine which food was responsible for the reaction? Take into consideration the following information. Allergic food reactions sometimes occur many hours after eating. The reaction might be caused by a combination of foods. The body can develop an allergy to a food to which it was previously immune.

3. The federal government regulates the collection of pollen. Pollens are the way some species reproduce. If too much pollen is collected from some species, they may become extinct. Have students formulate a "policy" of regulation for pollen collecting that is both "fair" to business and yet ecologically sound.

Turtle Tears

Have you ever seen a turtle cry? Well, not all of them do. Sea turtles shed tears when they come up on shore to lay their eggs. Are they sad to leave their babies? They don't take care of them, you know. Or is something else going on here?

TEACHER'S KEY

Puzzle: "Turtle Tears" — Why does a sea turtle cry when it leaves its eggs on shore to hatch?
Key Cognitive Skills: Hypothesizing, fact-finding
Key Concepts: Osmosis, chemical equilibrium
Difficulty Level: Moderately Difficult
Sources of Information: See references 1, 30, and 51 (for the second suggested additional activity).

Background Information and Solution

The problem in this puzzle is one of an animal that is adapted to one environment but must spend a portion of its time in another environment. The sea turtle is highly adapted to life in the sea.

This adaptation means its internal salts are in equilibrium with the high salt content of sea water. When the turtle comes on shore, a non-salty environment, it must reduce its internal salt concentration. The mechanism that the sea turtle uses to reduce the salt content is shedding tears.

Students may be helped through this problem by "working backward." Begin by asking students to consider the "purposes" of tears — relieving emotions, removing foreign substances from the eyes, secreting salts, and so forth. The teacher at this point may wish to give students a hint: These turtles also "cry" at times when they are in the ocean. Then ask which hypotheses are eliminated by this fact. If the only hypothesis that remains is "secreting salts," then ask students to explain why the turtle would need to remove excess salts. Absorption of salt through the skin from sea water causes salts to build up internally.

Alternate Hypotheses

1. The turtle gets sand and wind in its eyes when coming on shore. Have students research facts about the anatomy of the turtle's eye.

2. The turtle is upset at having to leave its offspring on shore. This hypothesis is a common suggestion from students and should not be taken too lightly. The question of whether animals have emotions is controversial and itself an emotional topic. See Suggested Additional Activities for exploring this topic.

SUGGESTED ADDITIONAL ACTIVITIES

1. Some scientists have completely ignored areas of inquiry because they are "impossible" to study. Such areas include animal intelligence, animal emotions, and animal pain. What are the difficulties in studying these areas? Can the difficulties be overcome? Have students discuss this topic. See reference 67.

2. Crying in humans has been recently studied but is still considered somewhat "mysterious." Do humans cry in order to eliminate salts? To believe this fact one would have to suppose that we become emotional when our salt balance goes awry. Why do we cry when we laugh too hard or when we peel an onion? How would one answer questions such as these? How would you collect tears in order to study them? Discuss the following question in light of the above questions: It is possible to have a science of human emotions? See references 30 and 51.

3. "Anthropomorphism" is the term used to describe the act of attributing human characteristics to a nonhuman object, including living things. Some scientists think that anthropomorphism should be taboo in scientific research regarding animals. It can lead us astray sometimes in studying an animal, can't it also be helpful in suggesting lines of inquiry? Bring a small animal to class and have students write sketches of the animal's behavior for a short period of time. As students read their sketches out loud, have the class try to identify statements that are anthropomorphic and discuss the relative validity of those statements.

Mosquito Control

Mosquitoes aren't just a nuisance. They can be very dangerous! They carry some very serious diseases. Unfortunately, using pesticides to control mosquitoes also can cause many serious problems. But maybe some ways can be found to control mosquitoes without using pesticides.
What do you think?

TEACHER'S KEY

Puzzle: "Mosquito Control"—Can students find a better way to control mosquitoes than using pesticides?
Key Cognitive Skills: Fact-finding, applicating
Key Concepts: Predation, life cycles
Difficulty Level: Moderately Difficult
Sources of Information: See references 24, 27, and 67.

Background Information and Solution

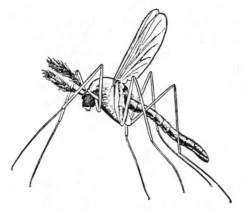

This problem does not have just one solution. Encourage students to collect as much information as they can on the life cycle of the mosquito and its natural history. What does it eat? What animals prey on mosquitoes? Where does it live during various stages of its life cycle? Once a sufficient amount of information has been collected, have the students apply strategies to interrupt the life cycle naturally —perhaps by introducing a predator or eliminating water sources. However, as students suggest different strategies, they should also attempt to predict consequences of changing certain features of the mosquitoe's environment. Suggestions should be practical and efficient, but not too costly

SUGGESTED ADDITIONAL ACTIVITIES

1. "Organic" agriculture and pest control are coming into prominence as alternative methods of dealing with nature. Using solutions to this puzzle as models, have students state a general

Libraries Unlimited, Inc. • P.O. Box 3988 • Englewood, CO 80155-3988   *Nature Puzzlers* (Lawrence E. Hillman)

"strategy" for developing organic controls. Ask them to create "principles" from these strategies. For example, the first principle might be "Always investigate the life cycle of the animal or plant in question."

2. A number of years ago, DDT was found in Arctic penguins. The DDT in these penguins originated from agricultural and pest control uses in the United States. Have students research and trace the flow of DDT from a farmer's field to the penguin, making as many connections as possible. As a start, tell the students that the DDT washes into the ground water first and travels to the ocean through the stream and river systems.

3. Have students brainstorm some organic methods of control for house pests—roaches, silverfish, mice, and so forth—and write a proposal for a loan to start a new business. This exercise works well if students work in groups to form the proposals, name their new companies, create market strategies, and so forth.

Straight and Narrow

When you look at a bunch of trees in a forest, you usually see trees of different sizes. Some are big, some are small, and some are "middle-aged." But when you go into a forest of lodgepole pines, one of the first things you notice is that the trees are all about the same size. This observation is true no matter what the age of the trees. If the stand of trees is young, you see all small trees—no larger ones. If the stand is middle-aged, you see all middle-aged trees—no saplings. All the trees are the same height and width, growing close together on dry soil covered with pine needles and cones. The trees are so close together, in fact, that you would probably have difficulty walking through them. You would be snagged with dead branches. And you would always be ducking under dead trees that didn't fall to the ground because there wasn't any room to fall.

The lodgepole pine forest has a real mysterious feel to it. Part of that mystery is why they all grow to be the same size.

Libraries Unlimited, Inc. • P.O. Box 3988 • Englewood, CO 80155-3988   *Nature Puzzlers* (Lawrence E. Hillman)

TEACHER'S KEY

Puzzle: "Straight and Narrow" — Why do lodgepole pines have a strange growth pattern?
Key Cognitive Skills: Deduction
Key Concepts: Fire as an ecological factor, adaptation, species survival
Difficulty Level: Moderately Difficult
Sources of Information: See references 13, 49, and 71.

Background Information and Solution

All the clues necessary to solve this puzzle are in the puzzler itself. The problem for the students is to find the common connection among all the factual elements: dense growth, dry soil, dry soil covering, dead branches, and dead trees standing nearly upright. All of these elements illustrate one common factor — fire potential.

Lodgepole pine reproduction is nearly impossible without fire. The seeds from cones will not germinate on the dark forest floor. They need bright sunlight. When a forest fire occurs, the trees in the forest are, of course, largely destroyed. The intense heat of the fire opens the cones of the lodgepole pine and the new seeds germinate in the sunlight and mineral enriched soil. Since the seeds germinate at relatively the same time and grow at a relatively constant rate under similar conditions, the trees are fairly uniform in height.

Alternate Hypotheses

1. All the pines grow from a single underground root so they all grow to the same height at the same rate. Some trees do grow from a single underground system. This system requires some time to develop. Therefore, some trees get a "head start" on others making for an uneven stand of trees.

2. Deer, elk, or other animals eat the saplings so only the other trees continue to grow to their maximum height. This hypothesis could be true if an area is over-grazed. The fact that no saplings are seen at all (unless the stand is made up entirely of saplings) makes this hypothesis unlikely.

SUGGESTED ADDITIONAL ACTIVITIES

1. Have students read articles about the recent fires in Yellowstone National Park — articles that were written during the fire and after the fire subsided. How accurate were the scientists' predictions? Did all scientists agree as to the ecological outcome of the fires? Did all scientists agree on what should be done about the fires? Debate the National Park Service's current policy toward man-made fires and natural fires. See resources 49 and 71.

2. The aborigines of Australia have used controlled burning of grasslands for thousands of years as a means of sustaining wildlife and plant populations. How is this practice advantageous to the aborigines? How many animals die? How can burning be done without endangering the area? How would you do it? When would you do it? How often would you do it?

3. One nature writer commented that the lodgepole pine seems to encourage its own destruction in order to ensure the survival of the species. This statement also is true for animals whose behavior might be self-destructive to the individual but beneficial to the group—the attack behavior of bees and ants, for instance. Could it be (as has been suggested) that genetic material has a "mind of its own" that works to preserve the species but cares nothing for the individual? How could such a proposition be proven? What facts would one be willing to accept as proof of this proposition? Why is this idea disturbing to us? Debate this unusual idea in class from as many perspectives as possible.

🍁 Hitchhikers 🍁

One city in the United States has more species of plants than any other city. But the plants were not put there on purpose; they hitchhiked.

What city do you think this is?

TEACHER'S KEY

Puzzle: "Hitchhikers"—How did so many plants get into this one city (unintentionally)?
Key Cognitive Skills: Deduction, questioning, assuming
Key Concepts: Seed dispersal
Difficulty Level: Moderately Difficult
Sources of Information: See references 25 and 33.

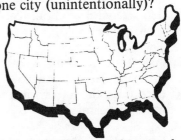

Background Information and Solution

Students quickly learn that sheer guessing will not reveal the solution. The puzzle must be approached in a systematic way. A number of possible ways exist for solving the puzzle, but students must at least narrow their options to several categories.

1. Encourage students to obtain information on seed dispersal and then decide which of these methods of dispersal is the most likely to be the "hitchhiker" method. Answer: seeds travel by wind, others pass through the digestive tracks of animals, some attach to clothing, and so forth.

2. Students must then brainstorm some possible methods of "transportation" that lead to particular destinations across the country. Answer: travel by air, automobile, trains, boats, and so forth.

3. Students must narrow the dispersing agent to one that is most likely to carry seeds and have a central terminal. Answer: travel by trains and boats.

4. Which of these choices are most likely to pick up the most seeds? Answer: trains and boats.

5. Which of these options is most likely to have a central terminal that is appropriate as a habitat for plants? Answer: trains and train yards.

6. What cities in the United States have the most extensive railway yards? Answer: St. Louis and Chicago.

7. Which of these two cities provides a more favorable climate for a variety of plants? Answer: St. Louis.

Alternate Hypotheses

Students can formulate practically an infinite number of possible hypotheses to initiate their search strategies. The teacher should remind students to begin with tentative hypotheses that indicate directions for inquiry, but to formulate hypotheses in terms of questions that allow them to judge the usefulness of a certain approach.

SUGGESTED ADDITIONAL ACTIVITIES

1. Research the structure of a variety of seeds. Collect actual seeds if possible. Seeds of various weeds are particularly interesting to examine. Have students describe the structure of these seeds and make hypotheses as to how they are distributed in the field. Test the seeds for flight or their ability to stick to clothing or fur. Group seeds according to the method of dispersal and have students generalize about features in each group. Encourage students to research the seeds to verify their predictions.

2. Ask students to draw the "ideal" seed. This seed should be capable of being dispersed in many different ways—by wind, water, hitchhiking, and so forth. When students have drawn the seed, encourage them to write a short description of the seed's structure and the function of each part in its dispersal.

3. Present the following problem to your class. One day you look in your notebook and discover a phone number, but there is no name beside it. You wonder who's number it is, so you decide to call. The phone, however, has been disconnected. Develop a search strategy to find out who the number belonged to.

4. Have students write a brief description of a close friend. The description should include the person's physical description, city and state in which he or she now resides, his or her hobbies, his or her jobs, and so forth. Then present this problem: Your friend mysteriously disappears, but there is no evidence that foul play is involved. All you know is that your friend has stayed within the state. How would you find your friend?

🍁 Dating Game 🍁

The tree stump shown below was cut in 1987. What was the climate like in 1980 in the area where this tree was cut? Was this tree cut as part of a logging operation?

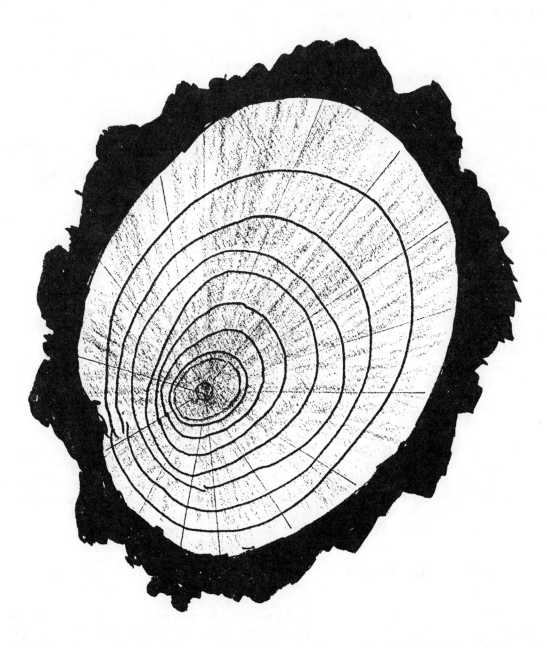

Libraries Unlimited, Inc. • P.O. Box 3988 • Englewood, CO 80155-3988

Nature Puzzlers (Lawrence E. Hillman)

TEACHER'S KEY

Puzzle: "Dating Game"—What kinds of information can be obtained from tree rings?
Key Cognitive Skills: Assuming, fact-finding, deduction
Key Concepts: Structure and growth of plant stems
Difficulty Level: Moderately Difficult
Sources of Information: See reference 56.

Background Information and Solution

The determination of a tree's past history from its growth rings is a very complicated process. The purpose of this puzzle is to encourage students to make some simple assumptions about tree growth and its relation to environmental factors.

In order to answer the first question in the puzzle, tell students that each growth ring represents one year's growth. Point out that this assumption can sometimes be false—trees sometimes grow more than one ring in a year (see Alternate Hypotheses). If we assume that this assumption is true, however, then we can count seven rings from the outside and find the growth ring for 1980. How is this ring different from the rest? The ring narrower than the others. If we assume that low moisture causes reduced growth, then we can deduce that a drought probably occurred during 1980. How can we justify this last assumption?

In order to answer the second question of the puzzle, we must try to imagine what would happen to the growth rings of a tree if nearby trees were cut. We deduce that if nearby trees were cut, the growth rings on one side of the tree would be larger than those on the other side. How can we justify this assumption? Since this growth pattern is shown, we can deduce that the tree was part of a logging operation.

Alternate Hypotheses

1. Factors other than low moisture cause reduced growth. This hypothesis is true. An insect infestation that destroyed the leaves could have been responsible for reduced growth. However, the fact that an insect infestation occurred during only one year and not in successive years is unlikely. Therefore, we will assume that insect infestation is not the cause of reduced growth.

2. A tree could grow more than one ring in a year and would throw off the calculation of the tree's age. This hypothesis is true. Trees can have "false rings." False rings occur when a drought or some other factor causes the tree to stop growing temporarily and then begin growing again when the conditions have improved. This growth pattern can produce two rings in the same growing season. Therefore, our first assumption may not be justified. We can only approximate the year in which the drought supposedly occurred.

SUGGESTED ADDITIONAL ACTIVITIES

1. Tree rings are often used to approximate the age of structures built by prehistoric humans. For example, beams from ancient dwellings are cut to expose tree rings. The rings are then used to date the structures. Have students brainstorm ways of using these beams to tell the age of buildings. Students usually just say to count the rings. Remind them that this will give only

the age of the tree used to make the beam, not the age of the building itself. The way the age of the building is determined is to count the rings in the beam and compare them with rings of trees still growing in the area. The rings of trees living during comparable time periods are so distinctive that they can be compared fairly easily by an expert. For example, assume that the outer rings of the beam match identically with the inner rings of the freshly cut tree. To find the age of the beam, count the rings from the outer edge of the freshly cut tree until the rings are identical with the ones in the beam. Then count the rings in the beam. Adding the two numbers together gives the age of the ancient building. Encourage students to research the culture of ancient people who used trees in the construction of their buildings.

2. What additional assumptions do you have to make to determine the age of an ancient dwelling? Discuss this question as a class.

3. In order to do science (or history, economics, geography, even just plain living from day to day), we have to make some assumptions. For example, the science of geology would be nearly impossible if geologists did not assume that the laws of physics and chemistry were the same in the past as they are today (the Uniformity of Nature Principle). Economists must make assumptions about "human nature." How are such assumptions justified? Have the class list the assumptions of the discipline you are now studying (geography, reading, etc.) and examine how these assumptions might be justified by facts, by other assumptions, and so forth. Do the same exercise with assumptions we make in everyday life.

Libraries Unlimited, Inc. • P.O. Box 3988 • Englewood, CO 80155-3988   *Nature Puzzlers* (Lawrence E. Hillman)

The Jacques Cousteau Beetle

Here's something you have to see to believe! I have a friend, Tom, who has an aquarium in his room with fish and other animals from the pond down the street. He keeps the aquarium "natural" —no air pumps or food dispensers. But that's not the weird part.

One day I was watching the animals in the aquarium and I saw a big beetle swimming around with the fish. After awhile I noticed that the beetle never came up for air—I mean never!

When I asked Tom about the beetle he said, "Yeah, I call him Jacques Cousteau. I don't know how he stays under water like that. I guess he has gills like a fish."

I wasn't going to be satisfied with that answer so I took a closer look. The beetle didn't have gills. In fact, it looked just like any other beetle! I still haven't figured out how the beetle managed to breathe, but I'm working on it.

Libraries Unlimited, Inc. • P.O. Box 3988 • Englewood, CO 80155-3988   *Nature Puzzlers* (Lawrence E. Hillman)

TEACHER'S KEY

Puzzle: "The Jacques Cousteau Beetle" — How can a beetle live under water without coming up for air?

Key Cognitive Skills: Hypothesizing, fact-finding

Key Concepts: Osmosis, adaptation

Difficulty Level: Moderately Difficult

Sources of Information: See reference 1.

Background Information and Solution

The solution to this puzzle has two parts. First, students must solve the problem of how the beetle carries its own air supply. Second, they must solve the more difficult problem of explaining why the air supply never runs out.

The solution to the first part is relatively easy: the beetle carries a bubble of air from a trip to the surface. This bubble of air surrounds the beetle's abdomen like a diving bell. Insects do not breathe in the same way that humans do. Their breathing tubes are located on the sides of their abdomens. Therefore, the beetle needs to carry the bubble around the lower part of its body.

But doesn't the bubble eventually run out of air forcing the beetle to resurface? The answer to this question is no. This part of the solution is the more difficult. As the beetle uses up oxygen in the bubble, waste gases build up in the bubble until the concentration of oxygen in the pond water is greater than that inside the bubble. When this imbalance of oxygen inside and outside the bubble occurs, oxygen diffuses into the bubble replenishing the supply.

Alternate Hypotheses

1. Oxygen from the water is absorbed through the beetle's skin. This hypothesis is a good try. But it is refuted by the fact that most of the beetle's "skin" is a hard, impenetrable exoskeleton.

2. The beetle breathes oxygen from the bubbles that form on the plants in the water. This hypothesis is also good, but is very unlikely considering the beetle's breathing apparatus.

SUGGESTED ADDITIONAL ACTIVITIES

1. The beetle in this puzzle is just one example of some remarkable — even unbelievable — adaptations to the environment. Have students research other examples of unusual adaptations in the animal world and report their findings to the class.

2. Some animals, such as whales, dolphins, and sea snakes, are air breathers but live in the water. What adaptations do these animals show that reflect their aquatic life? What generalizations, if any, can students make about adaptation to water life?

3. The beetle in this puzzle was able to carry air into a water environment. Do aquatic animals carry water with them into the air environment? Have students speculate on this possibility. Brainstorm ways that animals might do this, perhaps by writing a short description of the methods by which this could be done. Encourage students to research any animals that exhibit this behavior.

   Interestingly, some scientists speculate that land animals carry around a water environment called "blood." Debate the pros and cons of this speculation.

Libraries Unlimited, Inc. • P.O. Box 3988 • Englewood, CO 80155-3988   *Nature Puzzlers* (Lawrence E. Hillman)

Talking Trees

You probably thought that trees don't talk. Well, they do—sometimes. Here's how a scientist discovered this odd fact.

He placed a bunch of tent caterpillars on twenty wild willow trees. He was trying to find out if the willows would make poisons to fight off the caterpillars. A nearby group of willows didn't have any caterpillars.

About a week later, the scientist took the leaves from both sets of trees and tested them in his lab. Both groups of trees increased their poisons—even the ones that didn't have caterpillars!

The scientist figured that the infected trees sent a "message" to the uninfected ones. But he wasn't sure how they did it. So he took some potted willow trees to his lab and divided them into three groups of fifteen each. He took one group of willows to another building and just left them alone. He made sure, however, that they received the same amount of light, heat, and water as the other two groups. He kept the other two groups of willows in his lab. He put caterpillars on the trees in one group. He left the other fifteen trees alone.

Here's what happened. The trees in the other building did not produce any new poisons. But both groups of willows in the same room developed new poisons—even the ones that didn't have caterpillars on them.

The scientist concluded that the trees with caterpillars must have warned the other trees in the room. In other words, they must have "talked" somehow. What do you think?

Libraries Unlimited, Inc. • P.O. Box 3988 • Englewood, CO 80155-3988

Nature Puzzlers (Lawrence E. Hillman)

TEACHER'S KEY

Puzzle: "Talking Trees" — Do trees talk to each other?
Key Cognitive Skills: Most cognitive skills — particularly evaluating hypotheses and experiments
Key Concepts: Experimental method, scientific "proof"
Difficulty Level: Moderately Difficult
Sources of Information: See references 2, 48 (for third suggested additional activity), 57, and 66 (for fourth suggested additional activity).

Background Information and Solution

Note: Teachers should become familiar with the scientific method before attempting this puzzle, unless they plan to use it only for the purpose of hypothesizing.

The answer to this puzzle is still unknown. Student involvement in this puzzle has two objectives: to encourage them to evaluate the experiments described in the puzzle and to create hypotheses about the "causes" of the communication.

To evaluate the experiments, students should be at least somewhat familiar with the scientific method. Students unfamiliar with scientific experimentation can still learn something about this method if the problem is approached by formulating questions. Did the scientist prove that trees communicate? What other explanations exist for the experimental results? Could the scientist have improved the experiment? How? The point is to involve students in thinking through the problem of what it means to "prove" something in science.

Alternate Hypotheses

1. The uninfected trees were actually infected with another insect that the scientist did not see. This hypothesis may have been true. However, wouldn't the insects have affected the trees in the other building as well? The question is whether the scientist controlled as many variables as possible.

2. Trees communicate by chemicals underground through their root system. This hypothesis is also true. This type of communication does occur with some species of trees. But the scientist controlled this factor by placing the willow trees in separate pots.

SUGGESTED ADDITIONAL ACTIVITIES

1. A number of years ago, experiments were performed in which a lie detector was attached to plants in order to record electrical changes in their leaf surfaces. In another room, the experimenter dropped live shrimp into boiling water. According to the experimenter, the plants reacted with a "jump" in their electrical activity exactly at the moment the shrimp were "executed." Do these experiments "prove" that plants have feelings? How could these experiments have been done more precisely? Refer students to chapter 1 of reference 57.

2. Some researchers have found recently that plants subjected to drought emit high frequency sounds. Although humans cannot hear these sounds, apparently some insects can. The insects are attracted to these sounds and consume the plants. Does this fact "prove" that plants can communicate?

3. Discuss the following questions with the class:

    a. Can anything ever be proven absolutely in science?

    b. How can you be sure that a fact is true? Are there different types of facts?

    c. Can scientists disagree on facts? How and why? See reference 48.

    d. Can scientists disagree on theories? How and why?

    e. Why might scientists disagree on the results of an experiment?

4. Have students read a nonfiction book or article in which unusual claims are made—the appearance of ghosts, sightings of UFO's, and so forth. Ask students to identify the types of proof that are offered in the book for the claims made. How convincing is this proof? What types of proof would be acceptable? If students were making a similar claim, how would they prove it?

🍁 Green Dust 🍁

I skied to the bottom of the hill and waited for my friend, Jane, to round the corner of the mountain trail. Just as she came into view, she fell backward into a pile of snow. Fortunately, she fell near an aspen tree. Jane grabbed the tree and pulled herself upright.

"Yuk!" I heard her say.

I called up to her. "What's the matter? Are you hurt?"

"No," she said, "but I have this green dust all over my gloves."

"What is it?" I asked.

"I don't know, but it came off of this aspen tree," she said.

I rubbed my glove along the trunk of a nearby aspen. Sure enough, there was green dust on my glove too. "I wonder what it is?" I asked.

"I don't know. If it doesn't kill you, why wonder about it?" she asked.

The green dust obviously didn't kill me. But I have to admit, I still wonder about it anyway.

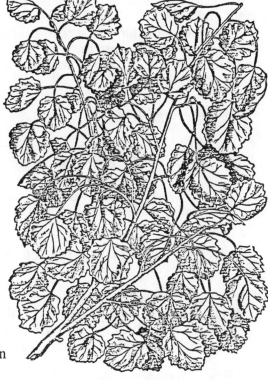

TEACHER'S KEY

Puzzle: "Green Dust"—What is green dust doing on an aspen tree?

Key Cognitive Skills: Deduction, hypothesizing

Key Concepts: Mutualism

Difficulty Level: Moderately Difficult

Sources of Information: See references 53 and 68 (for fourth suggested additional activity).

Libraries Unlimited, Inc. • P.O. Box 3988 • Englewood, CO 80155-3988   *Nature Puzzlers* (Lawrence E. Hillman)

Background Information and Solution

The main clue in this puzzle is the word "green." This word indicates—in a natural situation anyway—the chlorophyll of a plant. Could this green dust be a tiny plant? What type of plant? The green dust is algae, a tiny plant. Why would algae be growing on the side of a tree? What would be any benefit to the algae or to the tree for that matter? The algae obtains direct sunlight on the lower, branchless trunk of an aspen. In turn, the trunk of the tree is protected from the harsh ultraviolet rays of the sun at high altitudes.

Students can be "led" through this puzzle by having them focus on key clues. The snow, trail, and forest growth indicate that these people are probably in a wilderness area high in the mountains. The green color of the dust indicates a type of plant. The fact that the dust comes off easily from the trunk indicates that it is not a parasitic plant.

The point of this puzzle is to concentrate on making deductions from the clues given. The deductions do not have to be "true" since the clues are somewhat ambiguous. The puzzle also contains many "implied" clues. Encourage students to recognize some of these clues.

Alternate Hypotheses

1. The green dust is a residue produced by the tree. This hypothesis is worth researching in the library media center.

2. The green dust is a form of pollution. Ask students to research types of pollution that could cause trees to collect a green dust.

SUGGESTED ADDITIONAL ACTIVITIES

1. Have students read a short detective story that provides clues in a piecemeal fashion. Ask students to list the clues as they occur and make tentative deductions and hypotheses from these clues. As new clues appear, have students evaluate their hypotheses on the basis of the new evidence. Repeat the procedure as necessary.

2. Have each student make a collection of "brainteasers" that involve making deductions from a set of clues. Ask each student to present his or her puzzle to the class and guide the other students through the deductive process.

3. What "guests" does the human body support—that is, organisms that are just "along for the ride?" Are the organisms in our body beneficial or harmful? Encourage students to begin their research into these two questions by referring to reference 53.

4. Ask students to read reference 69. How does this "feather detective" use clues from feathers to deduce the species of bird that lost the feather? Is her process of reasoning "scientific"?

Nature Puzzlers III
Difficult

 Body Heat

You probably know that mammals and birds have constant body temperatures. Of course, different species of animals have different body temperatures. But nearly all species with constant body temperatures have one thing in common—their body temperatures are much higher than the average temperature of the environment.

Wouldn't it be easier on the animal to have a temperature lower than the environment—or at least the same as the environment?

TEACHER'S KEY

Puzzle: "Body Heat"—Why are the body temperatures of mammals and birds generally higher than the environment?

Key Cognitive Skills: Deduction

Key Concepts: Body temperature and environment, body temperature and physiology

Difficulty Level: Difficult

Sources of Information: See references 1, 18, 23, 41, 43, and 47.

Background Information and Solution

The approach to this activity is "supposing a case." In other words, the teacher generally will begin with questions such as "Suppose that humans had to maintain a body temperature that is the same as the air temperature. How would our bodies be different from what they are now? How would our lives be different?" Consider also the case for keeping the body temperature below air temperature. Compare the conclusions from the above suppositions to having a body temperature higher than the environment.

Direct students in making the following conclusions from their observations. First, high temperatures produce a high metabolic rate and, therefore, greater activity during cold spells. Second, a high body temperature is easier to maintain in cold weather through insulating fur and fat, shunting blood from skin capillaries, and shivering than to constantly eliminate heat through perspiration or other cooling mechanisms that are less efficient. In fact, few mammals can live in air temperatures more than a few degrees above their body temperature, since the external heat tends to speed up metabolism producing more internal heat, which in turn requires more cooling.

SUGGESTED ADDITIONAL ACTIVITIES

1. Have students investigate the lives of desert animals and then discuss the following questions:

   a. Why are so many desert animals either reptiles or insects?

   b. How would a human survive in the desert for a long period of time?

   c. How have some mammals that live in the desert adapted to the temperature extremes, both behaviorally and physiologically?

2. Have students investigate the adaptations of wildlife in other environments that have extreme conditions—the Arctic, the Galapagos Islands, Death Valley, and so on. Based on their findings, have students draw some general conclusions about the relationship between physiology, behavior, and climate.

3. Apply the principles and conclusions drawn from activity to humans that inhabit extreme climates—the Himalayan sherpas, Arctic Eskimos, Australian aborigines, and so forth. Have students predict various physiological and behavioral differences among peoples of various climates. How might their cultures (language, religion, art, family life, and so forth) reflect differences in environment? Test these predictions by reading descriptions of these various peoples and their cultures.

❧ Mounds ❧

Some animals are pretty good engineers. Beavers build dams, birds build nests, and prairie dogs build tunnels.

Last May our science class went on a field trip to see a prairie dog colony. It was neat the way the prairie dogs watched us as we walked around in the field. They would sit up on top of the mounds at the entrances to their tunnels and squeak warning messages to each other. Each tunnel has at least two entrances.

One guy in the class, Jack, said he thought some mounds looked higher than others. The teacher said that some mounds are higher than others because the tunnels are longer and more dirt had to be taken out. Tony said he didn't think that was right (and the teacher looked a little angry). Another student, Sue, said that the height of the mounds seemed to have some kind of pattern. The mound at one end of a tunnel was always a different size than the mound at the other end.

We decided that we were going to prove that the teacher was wrong. How do you think we did it?

TEACHER'S KEY

Puzzle: "Mounds"—Are prairie dogs better engineers than we think?
Key Cognitive Skills: Applying, hypothesizing
Key Concepts: Behavioral genetics, animal architecture, air pressure, adaptation to predators
Difficulty Level: Difficult
Sources of Information: See references 9, 11, 21, 23, and 41.

Background Information and Solution

This puzzle has several solutions because the mounds serve more than one function. Teachers should make this fact clear before students begin hypothesizing. The teacher may also want to guide students initially by directing them to the problems that prairie dogs face—predation, water, vegetation for food, a safe burrow, and so forth. Then encourage students to begin brainstorming

Libraries Unlimited, Inc. • P.O. Box 3988 • Englewood, CO 80155-3988   *Nature Puzzlers* (Lawrence E. Hillman)

possible uses of the mounds. Students will ordinarily focus on the most obvious uses of the mounds (see Alternate Hypotheses). These hypotheses do not account for the height difference in the mounds, although they do explain the existence of them.

If students become overly frustrated with attempting to solve this puzzle, suggest a hint or two. Direct their attention first to the problems of living underground—for example, what problems do miners face in working underground? The two most obvious problems are obtaining fresh air and avoiding flooding. Students may have difficulty thinking of these answers. The next question, then, should be obvious: "How do the mounds help solve these problems?" Flooding is controlled by directing water away from the entrance. The height difference in the mounds at each end of the tunnel creates a slight, but important, difference in air pressure above the holes. This difference in air pressure is enough to keep fresh air circulating in the tunnel.

Alternate Hypotheses

1. The mounds are used by prairie dogs to spot predators in the grass. This hypothesis is true but does not explain why the mounds are different heights. If spotting predators were the only reason for the mounds, the mounds probably would be more uniform in size.

2. The height of the mounds is purely accidental; after all, some mounds are bound to be smaller than others. This hypothesis is an interesting "explanation"—a kind of null hypothesis—and should be taken seriously. Discuss with students ways of validating and refuting this explanation.

SUGGESTED ADDITIONAL ACTIVITIES

1. If you want to have some fun (and a little bit of a mess) try this activity. Have each student bring to class a bunch of grass and twigs from their backyards or the school grounds. Then tell them to build a nest from the debris. They quickly learn that building a nest is not at all easy. Students become quickly motivated to find information on how some birds build their nests. The key, of course, is building the initial foundation from which the rest of the nest can be constructed. Refer students to reference 55.

2. Have students research the architecture of a number of different animals and report their findings to the class. Many of these structures are extremely complicated. Have students describe an experimental design that would help determine if the construction of these complicated structures is learned or genetic.

3. Some studies on twins separated at birth have shown remarkable similarities in the twins' lifestyles and behaviors. Discuss the validity and implications of these studies for understanding human behavior. Can these remarkable similarities be attributable to chance? What assumptions do the studies make about human behavior? What other interpretations might the studies have besides the ones given? See references 3 and 46.

🍁 A Management Decision 🍁

What would you do? We had only a couple of years to go before all the grouse would be gone from the heather. We stopped hunters from shooting them, but the grouse population still declined. We trapped and removed the animals that ate grouse. That didn't work either; the grouse continued to die. We even set aside places as refuges so the birds could be safe from urban development. The grouse population still declined. We haven't got much longer before all the grouse will be gone. None of us have a clue about what to do next. Do you have any suggestions?

Libraries Unlimited, Inc. • P.O. Box 3988 • Englewood, CO 80155-3988

Nature Puzzlers (Lawrence E. Hillman)

TEACHER'S KEY

Puzzle: "A Management Decision" — Why does grouse population continue to die off despite all efforts to save it?
Key Cognitive Skills: Applying, extrapolating
Key Concepts: Carrying capacity, limiting factors in an ecosystem
Difficulty Level: Difficult
Sources of Information: See references 13, 23, 40, and 41.

Background Information and Solution

None of the measures described in the puzzle worked indicating that other, less obvious, forces are causing the decline in the grouse population. For instance, students may hypothesize that disease is a cause of the problem. As students hypothesize various causes of death, they should in turn attempt to provide remedies for the cause. The remedies should be feasible. For example, developing a vaccine and then administering it to all the birds would be too costly and impractical.

Sometime during the discussion describe heather to the students. Heather is a small evergreen shrub that grows in the English and Scottish highlands. It is usually the most abundant plant in the area and the area itself is called "the heather."

This problem was actually solved by a rather ingenious method. First, the heather was burned. The burning provided new growth that was easier to reach and more nutritious for the grouse. The open areas also provided sunning yards so that grouse could dry off after a rain — thus preventing respiratory ailments. Second, the old breeders were removed from the area so that younger, more productive birds could move into new territories. Although this procedure was used in reality, point out that it is not the only correct answer to this problem. The more hypotheses that students can devise, the better. The same is true for developing applications and consequences of their ideas.

Alternate Hypotheses

1. Grouse eggs were being destroyed by an insecticide that was being used in a nearby farm.

2. Grouse were being killed by poachers who went undetected by the wildlife managers.

SUGGESTED ADDITIONAL ACTIVITIES

1. Students usually have strong feelings about the hunting of wild animals. Have students write an essay on their feelings about hunting while addressing both sides of the issue.

2. Have individual students investigate information on one of their favorite wild animals — what it eats, what predators it might have, what diseases it falls prey to, where it lives, and so forth. When a sufficient amount of information has been collected on the animal, have students write a "management plan" for the animal describing the measures they would take to preserve the animal in the wild.

3. Have students read about a species of animal that is endangered and investigate the measures — political, economic, and ecological — that are being taken to prevent its extinction. Are the measures working? What else can be done to save the animal? How can public awareness of the animal's possible extinction be increased?

The Plant with Two Personalities

Gromwell is a plant that grows in open areas, such as meadows, in the Rocky Mountains. Sometimes it grows into a one-stemmed plant. Other times it grows into a bushy plant like the one shown here.

What could possibly cause a plant to grow in two different ways?

TEACHER'S KEY

Puzzle: "The Plant with Two Personalities"—Why does gromwell grow in two distinct forms?

Key Cognitive Skills: Fact-finding, deduction, assuming, hypothesizing

Key Concepts: Factors affecting plant growth, hormones, apical dominance in plants

Difficulty Level: Difficult

Sources of Information: See references 25, 33, and 57.

Background Information and Solution

Gromwell grows in meadows in the Rocky Mountains. Since the plant is herbaceous, small animals, such as rabbits, nibble on the plant. The most succulent part of the plant is its growing tip which contains most of the plant's growth hormones. These hormones regulate the growth of the plant apex, or tip, where most of the upward growth occurs. The presence of growth hormones in the plant's apex partially inhibits growth hormones in other areas of the plant. This growth pattern is known as apical dominance. If a rabbit nibbles on the growing tip, the plant loses the hormones in the apex area. Growth in the "branches" of the plant then assume a greater, more dominant, role in growth. Thus the plant grows into a bushy form. Point out that this theory is the current answer to this puzzle but has not been proven definitely. Students may come up with some fairly convincing hypotheses of their own—some of which may be better than this theory. The current theory is held because other plants (such as tulip trees) show similar variation that cannot be explained by genetic differences or other environmental factors.

Libraries Unlimited, Inc. • P.O. Box 3988 • Englewood, CO 80155-3988   *Nature Puzzlers* (Lawrence E. Hillman)

Alternate Hypotheses

1. An animal collected and buried some seeds in the same spot. This behavior does happen with the seeds of some plants and is, therefore, a fairly convincing possibility. This hypothesis should be investigated further. For example, what animal might eat gromwell seeds? Are the seeds edible? Does the bushy form have several different root systems? Have students make predictions from this hypothesis and test them through fact-finding.

2. When the plant grows in an area where it is crowded by other plants, it grows in the one-stemmed form. When crowding is not a problem, it grows in the bushy form. Again, this hypothesis is good; predictions from it can be tested in fact.

SUGGESTED ADDITIONAL ACTIVITIES

1. Use the library to research various factors that affect plant growth. In particular, have students research the affects of temperature, wind, sunlight, soil, competition from other plants, and growth hormones. See references 25 and 57.

2. Once some factors affecting plant growth are identified, hypothesize how these factors may affect the "bushiness" of a plant. Use brainstorming to come up with as many hypotheses as possible.

3. Play an "If ..., then..." game. "If" is a statement of hypothesis and "then" is a fact predicted from the hypothesis. For example, "If the so-called bushy plant is really just a bunch of single-stemmed plants growing together, then the plant should have more than one root system." As inferences are made, have the students check the predicted fact with known facts about the plant.

4. Students often make a considerable number of assumptions when dealing with this puzzle. Typically they assume the cause is external—sunlight, rain, and so forth. Sometimes they may focus entirely on the internal conditions of the plant, such as genetics. Rarely do they ever consider the possibility that the solution is a combination of these two factors. Explain to students the meaning of the word "assumption" and ask them to verbalize the assumptions that they are making. Which assumptions do they feel are justified and which might need re-examination?

🍁 Connections 🍁

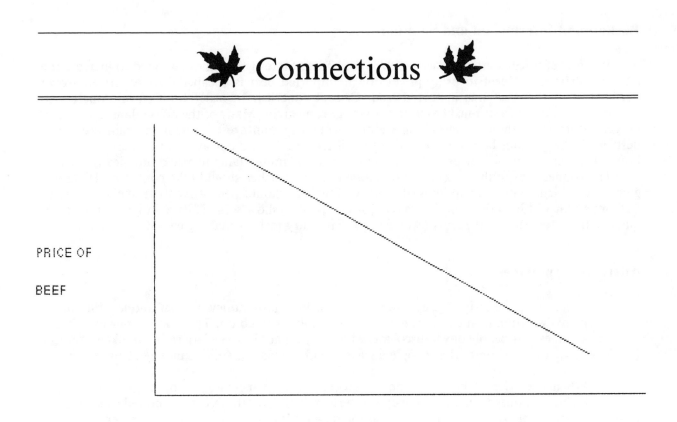

PRICE OF

BEEF

PRICE OF HOUSEPLANTS

The graph above shows a very definite connection between the price of beef and the price of houseplants. As the price of beef goes down, the price of houseplants increases. The relationship has nothing to do with individual supermarkets or chains. The connection goes much deeper than that.

What do you think is the reason for this connection?

TEACHER'S KEY

Puzzle: "Connections"—What kind of relationship exists between the price of beef and the price of houseplants?

Key Cognitive Skills: Deduction

Key Concepts: Ecological relationships, interference in ecosystems by humans

Difficulty Level: Difficult

Sources of Information: See references 13 and 17.

Background Information and Solution

When beef prices started to rise in 1978, the United States government decided to increase the amount of imported beef to bring prices down. Imported beef is cheaper than American-grown beef. Most of this beef was imported from Central America. In order for Central America to support cattle, rain forests must be cut to provide grazing areas. Many of the houseplants found in a grocery store or hothouse come from Central American rainforests. When the rainforests are destroyed, they cannot be regenerated due to soil erosion from the heavy rains. Therefore, fewer houseplants are available for export, causing the price of houseplants to rise dramatically.

The connections in this puzzle are so subtle that the teacher should take considerable care to guide the students into fruitful lines of inquiry. Teachers should help students frame appropriate questions that will help them in this task. However, try to show some reserve in giving too many hints as this often directs students away from the primary task of making causal connections.

Alternate Hypotheses

1. When the price of beef goes down, people spend more money on beef and less on houseplants which in turn causes the price of houseplants to go up. This guess is not bad, but it assumes that people buy houseplants when they do not buy beef—a rather unlikely connection. It also assumes that people always spend a constant sum of money at the store.

2. When the price of beef goes down, grocers have to increase the price of other things, including houseplants, to make up for the loss. This hypothesis can be refuted by two facts. First, the puzzle explicitly stated that the relationship was independent of grocers. Second, if the price of beef goes down, then the grocer pays less for the beef which may even increase the grocer's profit rather than cause a loss.

SUGGESTED ADDITIONAL ACTIVITIES

1. Research the destruction of tropical rainforests and, as a class, predict some consequences of this action for Central America in particular and the world in general.

2. What other improbable connections can students come up with? Take any item and trace a causal connection to some other item that seems unrelated. For example, "How is an automobile connected to a dinosaur?" (The gas in the car is made from oil that was produced by decayed plants and animals in the Age of Reptiles.) When individual students have found some improbable connections between two objects on their own, play a game with the class in which other students have to find the hidden links between the objects.

3. So-called "minute mysteries" are short puzzles that have an "obvious" solution as long as one is able to see an unobvious connection between two parts of the puzzle. For example, "A man walks into a restaurant and asks a waiter for a glass of water. The waiter, instead of providing the water, screams at the top of his voice. The man who asked for the water says a polite 'thank you' and walks out. Explain the man's behavior." In order to solve this puzzle, one must make an unobvious connection between a glass of water and a scream. The answer is that the man asking for the water had the hiccups and the scream scared him enough to stop them. Have students write some minute mysteries—either ones of their own or ones they have heard—and read them to the class.

Libraries Unlimited, Inc. • P.O. Box 3988 • Englewood, CO 80155-3988   *Nature Puzzlers* (Lawrence E. Hillman)

🍁 Seedy Business 🍁

Captain's Log, September 9, 1695

We made our way to the island of Mauritius this week to deliver our ship's load of livestock, mostly pigs. The ship's mascot, a black cat named Henry, managed to sneak off the ship while the crew was unloading. No one has found him yet; I don't suppose they will. I would rather see the Norway rats leave ship instead.

Captain's Log, September 11, 1695

The European settlers on the island are reporting a curious fact. One of the most abundant trees on the island (*Calvaria major*) is no longer reproducing. Hundreds of trees are littering the ground with seeds. And yet none of the seeds are sprouting into new trees. This situation is most odd. A ship's mate, who has been studying the plants on the various islands, says he has examined the seeds and finds them free from disease and insects. The soil still supports other native plant life, so we remain completely puzzled as to why this is happening.

TEACHER'S KEY

Puzzle: "Seedy Business" — Why do the seeds of an island tree boldly refuse to sprout?

Key Cognitive Skills: Assuming, deduction

Key Concepts: Factors in seed germination, extinction of species, effects of new species introductions, seed dispersal

Difficulty Level: Difficult

Sources of Information: See reference 10.

Libraries Unlimited, Inc. • P.O. Box 3988 • Englewood, CO 80155-3988   *Nature Puzzlers* (Lawrence E. Hillman)

Background Information and Solution

To solve this puzzle, students need to make the rather improbable connection between pigs, cats, and rats on the one hand and the seeds of a tree on the other hand. In presenting this puzzle, the teacher might point out that the livestock and other animals are responsible for the lack of seed germination. At first, students probably will suggest a number of direct connections (see Alternate Hypotheses). If students persist in attempting to make direct connections, suggest that they may be making an incorrect assumption—namely, that the causal chain has no intermediate link.

Encourage students to find out about animal factors in seed germination. When asked, for instance, about how some mammals disperse seeds, many students are familiar with the fact that animals eat fruits with seeds and that the seeds pass through the animal's digestive tract. The seeds are then dispersed through defecation. When further researching this question, students will discover that some seeds must pass through the digestive tract of an animal before the seed can germinate. The digestive juices break down a normally impermeable covering on the seed.

This characteristic is the key to the puzzle solution. The animal whose digestive system is necessary to make the seeds germinate is no longer around. It has been driven to extinction by the introduced carnivores. The extinct species in this puzzle is the famous dodo bird.

Alternate Hypotheses

1. The settlers had changed the soil by planting new crops. This hypothesis is fairly good because we know that this situation happens in the tropical rain forests of South America. In the puzzle, however, the tree is introduced to us as one of the most abundant trees on the island. Obviously, then, cultivation has not gone that far.

2. The seeds need shade in order to germinate and cultivation has removed the shade. This hypothesis also is fairly good. However, it explains only why some of the seeds are not germinating, not all of them.

SUGGESTED ADDITIONAL ACTIVITIES

1. Species of birds that live on islands seem to become extinct more often and more quickly than birds that live on continents such as Europe. Discuss some possible reasons for this situation. Birds able to move about freely on a continent and adapt to new locales are less likely to become extinct than birds that live on islands with nowhere to go.

2. Have students do research on the animals of Australia, perhaps dividing them into groups that cover certain topics. One group might report on marsupials, another on reptiles, and so forth. With this information in hand, ask students to predict, through chains of causal reasoning, what might happen if an American grey squirrel were introduced accidentally into Australia. Something similar to this did happen in Australia when rabbits were introduced there for the purpose of hunting. The rabbits overpopulated and created a huge nuisance, turning large areas into desert as a result of overgrazing. The introduction of rabbits also had an impact on other species that ate the same vegetation, which in turn had an effect on animals that preyed on the herbivores, and so forth. Encourage students to write their predictions as an "environmental impact statement."

3. Through genetics, scientists are attempting to create new life forms. Applying the lessons previously learned about introducing new species into an environment, discuss the ramifications of recombinant DNA research from an ecological point of view.

4. Discuss the "value" of species in the modern world. If species do not have any economic value, should they be allowed to become extinct? What obligations do humans have for saving species? Do animals have "rights"? Who should make decisions about the fate of animals? If you wanted to save a species, such as the gray whale, from extinction, how would you go about doing so?

Libraries Unlimited, Inc. • P.O. Box 3988 • Englewood, CO 80155-3988 *Nature Puzzlers* (Lawrence E. Hillman)

An Unlikely Story

Can a beetle put a monkeywrench into the theory of evolution? The beetle's life doesn't seem very significant … until you think about it.

This special beetle simply climbs up a mimosa tree and lays its eggs on a branch. The tree has to be a mimosa tree. This behavior is simple enough so far. But since its eggs can't survive in live wood, the beetle crawls on the branch toward the trunk of the tree for about a foot and then chews on the branch deeply enough to kill it. Soon the branch falls off and the beetle larvae feed on the dead wood. Later, the next generation of beetles is born.

Interestingly enough, this practice actually helps the mimosa tree. Without the beetle, the tree lives about thirty years. But if the beetle kills some branches—prunes the tree—the tree lives for nearly 100 years. Both the beetle and the tree benefit!

Now if this doesn't seem remarkable, think of it in terms of evolution. How in the world could all of this have evolved by chance? It seems rather unlikely, but perhaps you can find an explanation. As of now, this question is one of the great unsolved mysteries of biology.

Libraries Unlimited, Inc. • P.O. Box 3988 • Englewood, CO 80155-3988

Nature Puzzlers (Lawrence E. Hillman)

TEACHER'S KEY

Puzzle: "An Unlikely Story" — Can a beetle upset evolutionary thought?
Key Cognitive Skills: Most cognitive skills
Key Concepts: Theory of evolution
Difficulty Level: Difficult
Sources of Information: See references 5, 15, and 67.

Background Information and Solution

This puzzle is obviously an open-ended activity intended to be an introduction to mystery in nature. It is not intended to be a forum for the irrational proclivities of either evolutionists or creationists. This puzzle can be successful only for those who approach it with an open mind, because it raises questions about fundamental human beliefs. In this sense the problem is more "philosophical" than "scientific." The full range of cognitive skills may be evoked in the process — questions about assumptions, questions about logic, questions about questions, and questions about knowing and believing. All of these activities enrich the thinking skills of students. The teacher must be willing to cross academic disciplines and plunge head-on into fundamental issues. Those fearing the repercussions of either "hard-headed" colleagues or irate parents may wish to avoid this puzzle altogether.

SUGGESTED ADDITIONAL ACTIVITIES

1. Have students research and make a list of some true mysteries in nature. Which ones are more likely to be answered than others? How might the possible answers to these problems affect our knowledge of the world? How do the assumptions that we make about the world affect the way that we approach these problems? See references 15 and 67.

2. One way of interpreting this puzzle is to assume that the beetle is intelligent enough to figure out how to survive. If we make this assumption, however, it forces us to believe that the beetle knows something about water and mineral conduction in a tree. We also must believe that the beetle "understands" the growth requirements of its larvae (which it never sees after the eggs are laid). We also must believe that the beetle understands that tree pruning increases the tree's survival potential and connect this fact to its own survival potential. Is this too much to ask of a beetle? Do we have any rational reasons for believing that a beetle cannot have such intelligence? Can these same reasons be applied to humans as well? For example, the beetle exhibits many stereotyped behaviors, but then so do humans. How can we ever know that an animal is exhibiting intelligence as opposed to being an automaton? Have students debate this issue. See reference 5.

3. Have students read the accounts of scientists who have written about their own problem-solving activities. What part did luck, hunches, dreams, or logic play in their discoveries? Were these scientists all geniuses? Were some of them just ordinary people?

A Memory Like a Bird?

Suppose a teacher told you that this week's test would have 10,000 questions? You would probably complain that it's hard enough to remember ten things, let alone ten thousand. And yet, a certain kind of bird can remember that much! The Clark's nutcracker, a Rocky Mountain bird that eats seeds, can remember where it buried its winter supply of seeds, even if the seeds are hidden in 10,000 different places!

Does the bird really remember all of the sites or does it have a trick up its sleeve?

Libraries Unlimited, Inc. • P.O. Box 3988 • Englewood, CO 80155-3988   *Nature Puzzlers* (Lawrence E. Hillman)

TEACHER'S KEY

Puzzle: "A Memory Like a Bird?"—How can one explain the Clark's nutcracker's remarkable memory?
Key Cognitive Skills: Designing experiments, hypothesizing, deduction
Key Concepts: Experimental design, memory
Difficulty Level: Difficult
Sources of Information: Any good general psychology book.

Background Information and Solution

This puzzle does not have one specific answer; it is a completely open-ended exercise. Perhaps the best way to approach this puzzle is to have students design experiments on human memory—testing the effects of memory cues, nonsense syllable memorization, effects of organization, effect of meaning, and so forth. When some data have been collected and interpreted, have students draw analogies to the memory of the nutcracker. What cues might the bird use? What organization might exist in the burial of the seeds? As a further exercise, have students describe ways of testing these hypotheses in the field.

Alternate Hypotheses

1. The nutcracker buries its cache only at the base of certain species of trees.

2. The nutcracker is able to smell its buried cache of seeds.

SUGGESTED ADDITIONAL ACTIVITIES

1. Have students critique each other's or each group's experimental designs for studying human memory. Consider the following questions when doing the critiques:

    a. What assumptions were made? How can they be justified?

    b. Were variables controlled properly? Were all variables controlled except the one being tested?

    c. How were the data measured? How accurate were the measuring devices? Were all of the data quantitative? Were some qualitative?

    d. How was "memory" defined? Does the definition affect the way it is studied? Is there more than one type of "memory"?

    e. Are there alternate ways of looking at the data? What are other explanations for the results?

2. Have students read about the attempt to teach sign language to chimpanzees and apes. Review these studies on the same basis as activity 1 above. Refer students to references 5, 29, 54, 58, and 63.

🍁 The Left-Handed Minority 🍁

One of the many real mysteries that still remain in biology is why so many things in nature seem to be right-handed or show a right-handed sense. Take for instance the pattern of spirals in nature. Hawks, when they ride on rising thermals, tend to move upward in a right-handed spiral. The wood of trees near timberline in the mountains tends to grow in right-handed spirals. Bats, when leaving a cave, spiral in a right-handed direction. Sea shells often are formed in a right-handed spiral. How many people in your classroom are right-handed? Probably most of them!

But not all things are right-handed. Of all the things mentioned above, a few individuals are left-handed or move in a left-handed manner. The mystery, of course, is why things should be left-handed or right-handed anyway. Why shouldn't all humans be able to use both hands with equal ability? What difference would it make to a hawk whether it flew in a right-handed spiral or a left-handed spiral? Why should a snail care whether its shell is spiraling one way or the other? Why should right-handedness be chosen more often over left-handedness?

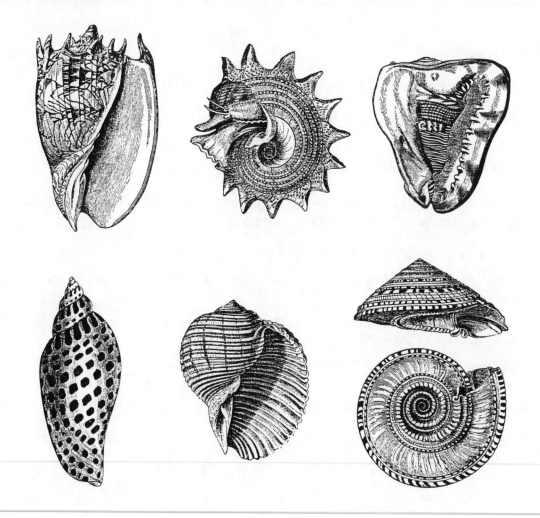

Libraries Unlimited, Inc. • P.O. Box 3988 • Englewood, CO 80155-3988   *Nature Puzzlers* (Lawrence E. Hillman)

TEACHER'S KEY

Puzzle: "The Left-Handed Minority"—What role does right- or left-handedness play in nature?
Key Cognitive Skills: All cognitive skills
Key Concepts: Variable according to emphasis
Difficulty Level: Difficult
Sources of Information: See references 37, 38, and 59.

Background Information and Solution

Have students make a collection of as many natural items as they can find that exhibit handedness. These items can include pine cones, shells, leaves, photographs of animals, the growth of vines, pictures of tornadoes, and so forth. Take a survey of students to determine their handedness. You may want to include in this survey questions such as "Which ear do you use to listen on the telephone?" "Do you have one eye that is stronger than the other?" and so forth.

Use this collection of handed objects to hypothesize, theorize, speculate, ask questions, and so forth about the nature of handedness. Is handedness genetic in humans, or learned? Do selective advantages exist for right-handedness? Does handedness have anything to do with the spin of the earth or the earth's magnetic field? How would you test such theories? Are molecules left-handed or right-handed? Is DNA a right-handed spiral? Do left-handed people have left-handed DNA?

The point here is that this inquiry is absolutely open-ended. It can take many turns and directions. In leading this inquiry, the teacher should focus on cognitive skills and not on subject matter. It is unlikely that students will "solve" this problem, although they may come up with excellent theories, concepts, questions, and so forth. Emphasize and reward their positive strides to becoming better thinkers.

Alternate Hypotheses

1. Handedness in nature is a response to the Coriolis force (due to the earth's spin) in the northern and southern hemispheres.

2. Handedness is a recessive genetic trait.

Off the Beaten Track

Our horses seemed nervous as we entered the clearing. In the nearby forest, only a squirrel could be heard chattering. Hank, my guide, brought his horse quickly to a stop. My horse, along with the two pack horses behind me, stopped in line.

"Is something wrong?" I asked.

Hank didn't answer. He got down from his horse, bent to the ground, and pressed his fist into some mud next to the trail. "Could be trouble, Bob," he said.

"What kind of trouble?" I asked, not sure I really wanted an answer. I quickly dismounted and tied the horses to a badly scarred tree. Then, I walked to where Hank was still kneeling.

"Grizzly," he said, pointing to a set of four tracks in the mud. "I know you came out here to see wildlife, but this is one you want to keep at a distance!"

"Why? Have you seen this bear before?" I asked.

"No. But I can tell you she is a female, nearly 400 pounds in weight, about three years old, and probably has at least two cubs with her. She also has an injury to her right shoulder. Since she is nearby, I think we should stay here until she moves on."

"Would you mind telling me how you know so much about this bear?" I asked.

"Sure," Hank said. "Just look and listen."

How could Hank learn that much information from a set of paw prints?

Libraries Unlimited, Inc. • P.O. Box 3988 • Englewood, CO 80155-3988   *Nature Puzzlers* (Lawrence E. Hillman)

TEACHER'S KEY

Puzzle: "Off the Beaten Track"—How much can you learn from a bear print?
Key Cognitive Skills: Most skills, particularly deduction
Key Concepts: Varies
Difficulty Level: Difficult
Sources of Information: See references 8 and 36.

Background Information and Solution

This puzzle is presented in the true spirit of inquiry—with all of its inherent uncertainty. Unfortunately, animal tracking cannot be made into an exact science with easy formulas. Fortunately, this makes animal tracking an ideal topic for inquiry. The point of the puzzle is to encourage cause-and-effect thinking of the broadest kind. The fact that there are no easy answers forces the student to examine many approaches and deduce consequences from various alternative viewpoints.

The following are rough outlines of possible solutions—they are not intended to be "the answer." Use these guidelines only as means to produce further inquiry and to stimulate further thinking.

1. Age of animal—Younger animals tend to make smaller tracks and take shorter strides. The texture of the heel pad tends to become rougher with age. Very young and very old animals tend to wobble in their gait since they are less steady on their feet. Using these types of data Hank was able to determine that this bear was quite young.

2. Sex of animal—In some species, such as the grizzly, the males tend to have broad shoulders and narrow hips. The opposite is true for females. Therefore, the hind tracks of the male tend to be closer to each other than the fore tracks—vice versa for the female. Also, the males of most species tend to place a little more weight on the outside of the hind feet (to ease pressure from the thighs on the external genitalia). Females tend to place the weight more on the inside of the hind feet. The depth of the track, therefore, on either side of a print is uneven and varies according to the animal's sex. Hank was able to use this information to tell the bear was a female.

3. Animal's weight—This guess is tricky because so many variables come into play. However, a good estimate can be made by a simple method. Hank exerts a known pressure with his fist into the mud (experience gained from many years of tracking) and estimates its depth. Using his fist mark as a gauge, Hank then estimates the pressure exerted by one paw. Since this is approximately one-fourth of the animal's total weight, he multiplies this figure by four to obtain the approximate weight of the bear. In order to make this method more effective, the tracker must have a great deal of experience with different soil consistencies and temperature conditions. Hank's experience told him the bear weighed about 400 pounds.

4. Hank figured the bear was injured in the shoulder by observing that the right paw print's depth was noticeably less than the other prints, but was made with an even distribution of pressure over the pad. The latter fact decreased the likelihood of a knee joint injury or a foot injury—both of which would have resulted in an uneven depth over the print.

Libraries Unlimited, Inc. • P.O. Box 3988 • Englewood, CO 80155-3988   *Nature Puzzlers* (Lawrence E. Hillman)

5.   The scars on the tree where the horses were tied are bear scratchings—a sign left by the bear to indicate its territory.

6.   The lone squirrel chattering in the distance was probably warning other squirrels of the bear's presence—although the squirrel may have spotted Hank and Bob.

7.   Hank knew that grizzlies become sexually mature at three years of age. Therefore, the bear probably had cubs.

SUGGESTED ADDITIONAL ACTIVITIES

1.   Hank made a series of hypotheses about the bear based on his limited observations. Have students suggest further observations of tracks or the nearby woods that would help Hank verify or refute his hypotheses.

2.   How could Hank's observations be made more scientifically exact? If his initial observations were more certain, would his conclusions be more certain?

3.   Experiment with human tracks in sand, mud, and soft soil. Collect data on height, weight, build, sex, and so forth and correlate them with depth of track, spacing of feet, and length of stride. Develop methods for making exact track measurements. Use the methods developed in class to predict the height and weight of a person making unknown tracks or tracks made by people in the class whose weight and height have not been measured. In other words, develop a "science of tracking."

References and Resources

1. Bannister, K., and A. Campbell. *Aquatic Life*. New York: Facts on File Inc., 1985.

2. Batten, A. "How Plants Fight Back." *International Wildlife* 18 (July-August 1988): 40-43.

3. Begley, S. "All about Twins." *Newsweek* 110 (November 23, 1987): 6-13.

4. Begley, S. "On the Trail of Acid Rain." *National Wildlife* 25 (February-March 1987).

5. Brownlee, S. "A Riddle Wrapped in Mystery." *Discover* 6 (October 1985): 85-93.

6. Connif, R. "The Ten Most Venomous Animals." *International Wildlife* 18 (May-April 1988: 18-25.

7. Cousteau, J. *Invisible Messages*. New York: Danbury Press, 1973.

8. Craighead, F. *Track of the Grizzly*. San Francisco: Sierra Club Books, 1979.

9. Curry-Lindahl, S. *Wildlife of the Prairies and Plains*. New York: Harry N. Abrams Inc., 1979.

10. De Roy, T. "When Aliens Take Over." *International Wildlife* 17 (January-February 1987): 34-37.

11. Ferrara, J. "Prairie Home Companions." *National Wildlife* 23 (April-May 1985): 48-53.

12. Ferrara, J. "Why Vultures Make Good Neighbors." *National Wildlife* 25 (June-July 1987): 16-20.

13. Friends of the Earth. *The New Environmental Handbook*. San Francisco: Friends of the Earth Books, 1980.

14. Garelik, G. "The Killers." *Discover* 6 (October 1985): 108-115.

15. Gilbert, S., et al. "The Greatest Unanswered Questions of the 20th Century." *Science Digest* 93 (October 1985): 34-61.

16. *Guinness Book of Remarkable Animals*. Edited by Ulla Sunden. Gothenburg, Sweden: Guinness Books, 1985.

17. Hair, J. "A Golden Deal: Debt for Nature." *International Wildlife* 17 (September-October 1987): 30.

18. Harrison, G. "Coping with the Cold." *National Wildlife* 26 (February-March 1988): 18-19.

19. Heinrichs, J. "There's More to Forests Than Trees." *National Wildlife* 26 (February-March 1988): 4-11.

20. Hemonick, M. "The Heat Is On." *Time* 130 (October 19, 1987): 58-63.

21. Honders, J. *The World of Mammals.* New York: Peebles Press, 1975.

22. Horan, K. "Dogging It Through the Wilderness." *National Wildlife* 24 (February-March 1986): 40-45.

23. Hylander, C. *Wildlife Communities.* Boston: Houghton Mifflin Co., 1966.

24. Jordon, W. "Bug Zappers that Don't." *Science 85* 6 (July-August 1985): 88.

25. Kister, R. *The World of Plants. Encyclopedia of the Life Sciences 3.* New York: Doubleday Publishing Company, 1965.

26. Lessen, D. "Here Come the Killer Bees." *National Wildlife* 17 (May-June 1987): 12-15.

27. Lewis, T. "Why the Mosquito May Be Winning the War." *National Wildlife* 24 (June-July 1986): 20-23.

28. Lewis, T. "High Stakes in a Land of Plenty." *National Wildlife* 25 (June-July 1987): 4-11.

29. Linden, E. *Silent Partners: The Legacy of Ape Language.* New York: Times Books, 1986.

30. Maranto, G. "Emotions: How They Affect Your Body." *Discover* 5 (November 1984): 35-38.

31. McCourt, R. "Creating Miniature Worlds." *National Wildlife* 18 (January-February 1988): 38-40.

32. McCourt, R. "Why Don't Animals Have Wheels?" *National Wildlife* 18 (May-June 1988): 40-41.

33. Milne, L. and M. Milne. *Living Plants of the World.* New York: Random House Inc., 1985.

34. Monmaney, T. "The Chemistry between People." *Newsweek* 109 (January 12, 1987): 54-55.

35. Morgan, D., and T. Monmaney. "The Bug Catalog." *Science 85* 6 (July-August 1985): 37-41.

36. Murie, O. *A Field Guide to Animal Tracks.* Boston: Houghton Mifflin Co., 1974.

37. Neville, A. "Symmetry and Asymmetry Problems in Animals." In *The Encyclopedia of Ignorance.* Edited by R. Duncan and M. Weston-Smith. New York: Pocket Books, 1977.

38. Olson, S. "Why Is Life Handed?" *Science 84* 5 (October 1984): 22.

39. Overbye, D. "The Theories of Cosmic Winter." *Discover* 5 (May 1984): 26-29.

40. Peterson, R. *The Birds. Life Nature Library.* New York: Time-Life Books, Inc., 1963.

41. Rabkin, R. and J. Rabkin. *Nature in the West*. New York: Holt, Rinehart & Winston, 1981.

42. Rensberger, B. "Nuclear Winter: The Storm Builds." *Science 84* 5 (September 1984).

43. Ricciuti, E. *Wildlife of the Mountains*. New York: Harry N. Abrams Inc., 1979.

44. Robbins, J., "When Species Collide." *National Wildlife* 26 (February-March 1988): 20-27.

45. Roberts, M. "A Light in Time." *Psychology Today* 21 (January 1987): 22.

46. Rosen, C. "The Eerie World of Reunited Twins." *Discover* 8 (September 1987): 36-42.

47. Sage B. *The Arctic and Its Life*. New York: Facts on File Inc., 1985.

48. Sapolsky, R. "The Case of the Falling Nightwatchman: In Behavioral Biology All Facts Are Not Created Equal." *Discover* 8 (July 1987): 42-45.

49. Satchell, M. "Burn Baby Burn. Stop Baby Stop." *U.S. News and World Report* 105 (September 19, 1988): 14-16.

50. Schneider, S. "Nuclear Winter: The Storm Builds." *Science Digest* 93 (January 1985): 48.

51. Schreiner, S. "Why Do We Cry?" *Reader's Digest* 130 (February 1987): 141-144.

52. Schwartz, D. "They Got Rhythm." *National Wildlife* 25 (December-January 1987): 34-37.

53. Simon, H. *Partners, Guests, and Parasites*. New York: Viking Press, 1970.

54. Starr, D. "This Bird Has a Way with Words." *National Wildlife* 26 (February-March 1988): 34-36.

55. Terres, J. "Building a Better Home." *National Wildlife* 25 (April-May 1987): 42-49.

56. Thybony, S. "Dead Trees Tell Tales." *National Wildlife* 25 (August-September 1987): 40.

57. Tompkins, P. *The Secret Life of Plants*. New York: Harper & Row Publishers Inc., 1973.

58. Toner, M. "Louis: The Talking Chimp." *National Wildlife* 24 (February-March 1986): 24.

59. Trefil, J. *Meditations at Ten Thousand Feet*. New York: Charles Scribner's Sons, 1986.

60. Turbak, G. "Prisoner of Geography." *National Wildlife* 25 (February-March 1987): 14-17.

61. Unkelback, K. *The American Dog Book*. New York: E. P. Dutton, 1976.

62. Wexler, M. "How Do You Judge a Pretty Face?" *National Wildlife* 26 (February-March 1988): 52-58.

63. Whiteley, H. "Be Hep to Your Pet." *Saturday Evening Post* 259 (September 1987): 70-71.

64. Williamson, L. "A Deadly Rain." *Outdoor Life* 179 (June 1987): 46.

65. Wilson, E. "Pheromones." *Scientific American* 128 (May 1963): 100-114.

66. Wingerson, L. "Training the Mind to Heal." *Discover* 3 (May 1982): 80-85.

67. Wolkomir, R. "Five Decades of Discovery." *National Wildlife* 25 (April-May 1986): 55-65.

68. Wolkomir, R. "Roxie Laybourne: Feather Detective." *National Wildlife* 26 (December-January 1988): 20-25.

69. Wolkomir, R. and J. Wolkomir. "Between a Rock and a Cold Place." *National Wildlife* 25 (June- July 1987): 46-51.

70. Wolkomir, R. and J. Wolkomir. "An Ode to Noses." *International Wildlife* 18 (July-August 1988): 44-50.

71. Zuckerman, J. "We Could Have Stopped This." *Time* 132 (September 5, 1988): 19.

Skills Index

Concept Index

Organism Index